Praise

SPOK

"A well-researched, invigorating celebration of a spirited art form." —*Kirkus Reviews*

"Wide-ranging. . . . Joshua Bennett [is] one of the genre's most exciting and knowledgeable writers." —CBS News

"While competing with his collegiate slam team at the University of Pennsylvania, Bennett absorbed a powerful lesson from a mentor. He learned that performance poetry could be interpreted as an 'insistence on his own survival.' That's a ringing endorsement for this art form, and this book." —*San Francisco Chronicle*

"A talented poet in his own right, Bennett turns his attention to tracing the lineage and celebrating the impact of spoken-word poetry in the U.S. . . . Composed in dynamic, interlocking scenes, the story unfolds effortlessly despite the scholarly rigor and research evident in the writing. . . . Bennett succeeds." —*Booklist*

"Bennett wasn't on the sidelines observing the spoken-word revolution—he was in it. . . . It is rare to find such a nuanced and erudite record from an insider of a culture. A must-read for all interested in poetry, culture and its evolution."
—Roger Robinson, author of *Home Is Not a Place*

"Anyone who has felt the heart-racing, heart-aching, heart-breaking atmosphere of a spoken-word venue; anyone who revels in the wordplay performance poets let reverberate on a page; poets who spit fire (of course, nothing less will do)—this is for you. Bennett captures lightning in a bottle."
—Therí A. Pickens,
author of *Black Madness :: Mad Blackness*

"A galvanizing, thoroughgoing history of rare literary quality. Bennett is courageously personal and honest in his account, but it's a passion which speaks to all of us, and to anyone still finding their voice or the nerve to take that risk, from the back room of the local arts center to the biggest stages in the world."
—Luke Kennard,
author of *Notes on the Sonnets*

"Bennett's memoir and cultural history is a stirring reminder that no other art form is grounded in, and centers, community like spoken word does."
—Rishi Dastidar, author of *Saffron Jack*

"Bennett's enthusiasm for the subject leaps off the page, highlighting the resilience and adaptability of poetry and making clear how important the collective is to its progress. It's a spirited introduction to a vibrant art form."
—*Publishers Weekly*

Joshua Bennett

SPOKEN WORD

Joshua Bennett is the author of *The Sobbing School*, which was a National Poetry Series selection and a finalist for an NAACP Image Award. He is also the author of *Being Property Once Myself, Owed,* and *The Study of Human Life*. He has received fellowships and awards from the Guggenheim Foundation, the Whiting Foundation, the National Endowment for the Arts, and the Society of Fellows at Harvard University. He is a Professor of Literature and Distinguished Chair of the Humanities at MIT.

drjoshuabennett.com

Also by Joshua Bennett

SPOKEN WORD

SPOKEN WORD

A Cultural History

Joshua Bennett

Vintage Books
A Division of Penguin Random House LLC
New York

FIRST VINTAGE BOOKS EDITION 2024

Copyright © 2023 by Joshua Bennett

All rights reserved. Published in the United States by Vintage Books,
a division of Penguin Random House LLC, New York and distributed
in Canada by Penguin Random House Canada Limited, Toronto.
Originally published in hardcover in the United States by Alfred A. Knopf,
a division of Penguin Random House LLC, New York, in 2023.

Vintage and colophon are registered trademarks
of Penguin Random House LLC.

The Library of Congress has cataloged the Knopf edition as follows:
Names: Bennett, Joshua (Poet), author.
Title: Spoken word: a cultural history / Joshua Bennett.
Description: First edition. | New York: Alfred A Knopf, 2023.
Identifiers: LCCN 2022027131 (print) | LCCN 2022027132 (ebook) |
Subjects: LCSH: Spoken word poetry, American—History
and criticism. | Performance poetry—United States—
History. | Poetry slams—United States—History.
Classification: LCC PS309.S77 B46 2023 (print) | LCC PS309.S77 (ebook) |
DDC 808.5/45—dc23
LC record available at https://lccn.loc.gov/2022027131
LC ebook record available at https://lccn.loc.gov/2022027132

Vintage Books Trade Paperback ISBN: 978-1-9848-9786-2
eBook ISBN: 978-0-525-65702-6

Author photograph © Rog Walker
Book design by Michael Collica

vintagebooks.com

Printed in the United States of America
10 9 8 7 6 5 4 3 2 1

For anyone and everyone trying to get free

A Note on Form

Spoken Word: A Cultural History is a book of many rooms. It is a story of pulpits and hymnals and congregants' pews, second-hand microphones, dimly lit pubs, and café tables built for four but seating six. It is an assemblage of voices so loud the neighbors complain as the open mic runs another hour past schedule, but the authorities are never called (as this conflict, from the very first, is understood to be simply another part of the performance). It is a grand historical relay across the twentieth and twenty-first centuries: a tale of chance encounters and lifelong friendships, raucous conflict and unfettered celebration, acted out across a thousand stages. At the level of genre, it is a work of narrative nonfiction, arranged as a set of interwoven scenes, all of which share a single, shimmering through line: the complex beginnings, and widespread contemporary influence, of spoken-word poetry in the United States of America.

There are several stops on this journey. Our story begins in New York City, between Miguel Algarín's Lower East Side living room—which served as the precursor to the Nuyorican Poets Cafe—and the pedagogical experiments of the Black Arts Movement uptown, and it eventually heads half-way across the country to the Get Me High Lounge in Chicago, Illinois, where, in a small, unruly performance venue, the first-ever poetry slams on record took place. The book closes in a room that is, in a sense, many rooms at once, a space beyond space: the countless computer and smartphone screens that now serve as the medium through which millions of people experience and fall in love with spoken word for the first time. My goal in structuring the book this way is not only to paint a robust picture of how a specific performance subculture came to be one of the most influential literary genres of our age, though that is certainly a matter of great importance to me personally. Rather, my aim here is to honor its spirit, and the way it shows up in the world. This book's configuration—at both the level of style and the use of the many individual voices of participants to help elaborate its arguments—is meant to echo the shape and tenor of the poetry which serves as its inspiration and condition of possibility. Thus, I will tell this story through a combination of the close reading of archival materials, autobiographical reflection, and interviews with living legends in the fields of poetry and performance. This method, like the organization of this book, emerges from my desire to relay a narrative that resembles, in flow and in form, the historical phenomena it describes. The living historical actors chronicled in this book show up in real time. They clarify, and concretize, and complicate the narrative. They are this book's chorus. They are its magnitude and bond.[*]

---

[*] I am borrowing this turn of phrase from Gwendolyn Brooks's poem "Paul Robeson." Both Brooks and Robeson will reappear shortly.

In telling the fifty-year story of how several, distinct collectives of poets, musicians, writers, teachers, academics, playwrights, novelists, and organizers defied expectations, were surveilled by the United States government, and ultimately gave us the sound we can now hear everywhere from mainstream radio to Broadway musicals to the underground performance venues where it all began, I hope to reclaim the political ethos and persistent dreaming of a moment that is both part of our shared past and still among us. In turning to this archive—and leaving as much living, breathing room for the voices in there to speak as they will—I hope to recover the larger human vision that these writers committed their lives to. At its core, *Spoken Word* is the song of their lifelong struggle and ultimate triumph. It is an homage, in paper and ink, to an origin story that once lived only in the air and the annals of memory: a collective, atmospheric account both of what we lost and what can never, ultimately, be destroyed.

Introduction

(prelude to a sermon on gathering)

Every historian of the multitude, the dispossessed, the subaltern, and the enslaved is forced to grapple with the power and authority of the archive and the limits it sets on what can be known, whose perspective matters, and who is endowed with the gravity and authority of historical actor.

—Saidiya Hartman, *Wayward Lives, Beautiful Experiments*

When you think back over all of our past lives, only poetry could best fit the vast emptiness created by men.

—Malcolm X, writing to his brother, Philbert, while incarcerated in Norfolk Prison Colony in 1949

Church was the hood Juilliard to me.

—Frank Ocean

It was the spring semester of 2009, and I was alone in my dorm room, looking over notes for my film class on Spike Lee, trying to connect *Malcolm X* and *Mo' Better Blues* in a way that felt entirely original. Blu & Exile's *Below the Heavens* played as loudly as my second-generation MacBook would allow. I was a newly minted double major in English and Africana Studies at the University of Pennsylvania, nearing the end of my junior year. I lived in the W. E. B. Du Bois College House: a dormitory at the edge of Penn's campus named for the philosopher, sociologist, novelist, and poet. Though Du Bois himself had a truly harrowing time as a faculty member at the university back in 1896—he was allowed neither to have an office nor to teach students during his time at Penn—the dormitory was as robust a reflection of human life on Earth as one might hope to see on a college campus: students from all over the world, mostly black and brown, choosing to live in this place for its emphasis on social justice, the arts, and the celebration of cultural practices from across the African diaspora.

It was in this *uniquely* boisterous environment—surrounded by the charismatic boasts of hip-hop and dancehall, the steel boom of soca and kompa, hallways filled with laughter and conversation—that I looked up from my notes to see a missed call from a California area code. Whoever it was had left a voicemail message. I turned down the music and put my ear to the phone. The voice on the other side belonged to James Kass, founder and executive director of the nonprofit poetry organization Youth Speaks. Without much in the way of lead-up, and with a tone of palpable joy in his voice, James had asked if I would be interested in reciting one of my poems at the White House. I would have to agree to a thorough background check and be ready to go within the next week.

I can still remember looking at the phone, and then at the ceiling, and then at the desk across from my twin bed, covered with textbooks and printed notes. For a while I just sat there, frozen. I returned James's call, and after what might have been the shortest round of small talk in my entire life ("Hi, James, it's Josh—got your message. What's going on now, exactly?"), we got to the matter of the voicemail. James told me that if I was interested, I would have the chance to recite my original work in the East Room, alongside various literary and dramatic luminaries. He had no other information to share at the time (which was fine with me, given how strong the opening pitch was) and instructed me to stay by the phone. In a few minutes, I received a call from Stan Lathan, who laid out all the details.

At this point, I had known Stan personally for a little over a year, though I was familiar with his work from a childhood spent watching it with family and friends. Over the course of his career, he had amassed directorial and production credits for *Def Comedy Jam, Def Poetry, Sister Sister,* and *Martin* along with numerous other black American televisual touchstones. In 2008, he produced an HBO documentary called *Brave New Voices,* which featured poetry slam teams from across the country as they were headed to an international youth slam competition by the same name. Back when I was a freshman at Penn, I'd earned a spot on the Philadelphia team that won the 2007 Brave New Voices title: a mélange of college students from Philadelphia-area schools and teenagers from around the city, with styles ranging from lyric poetry straight from the page to verses that called upon the cadence of the hip-hop styles that raised us. In 2008 we were set to return to BNV, hoping for a repeat performance. Weeks before the trip, we learned that the entire competition, as well as the road leading up to it, would be filmed by HBO. Our team was one of five that would be featured in a soon-to-be-televised documentary. For the better part of three months, the cameras followed us everywhere: across our respective campuses, and even to the neighborhoods we grew up in. They recorded our weekly practices, as well as our fundraising efforts on the streets of West Philadelphia: hours spent performing poems in shifts at the intersection of 40th and Walnut, right in front of the movie theater, my red New Era fitted cap left upside down on the sidewalk to collect cash donations from passersby.

After the *Brave New Voices* documentary aired, Stan helped create all sorts of other opportunities for me to share my work with the world. Three months before the White House event, he invited me to perform at the 2009 NAACP Image Awards in Los Angeles. Now he was inviting me to DC, only this time I would be the only one onstage. No friends or teammates—just me, and the microphone, and one of the hundred poems I had scrawled into various black-and-white notebooks over the years. According to Stan, for the event in question, *An Evening of Poetry, Music, and the Spoken Word,* I was to recite a new, original work—a two-minute poem, to be exact—on the theme of communication. The audience would include President Obama and the first lady, Michelle Obama. I thanked him for the opportunity and hung up the phone.

After the call, I ran laps around my dorm—and not my dorm room, to be clear, but the entirety of the Du Bois College House—for the next ten minutes. It took me a day or two, but I eventually settled on the poem I would read: "Tamara's Opus," an ode to my older sister. The subject of the poem was my relationship with Tamara, who is deaf, and by extension my relationship to American Sign Language, which I had struggled to learn as a child. Given the theme, and the stakes of the moment, I knew there was no other poem I could share from that stage. If I had an audience with the president, even if it was just for two minutes, this was the message I wanted to leave with him.

The trip to DC was surreal. I had never ridden an Amtrak train before, and this ticket had come courtesy of the executive branch. I reclined my chair and tried to take a nap, but was too anxious. And so, as has become my custom during the decade since that trip, I rehearsed my poem, backwards and forwards, as many times as I could. The version I would be performing at the White House had been edited for time and was now two minutes flat (as opposed to the three-minute-fifteen-second version of the poem I'd performed during a showcase at Penn the year before). The new version was somewhat unfamiliar, but still felt true to the spirit of the original. To this day, "Tamara's Opus" stands out among all the poems I have ever written—not only because it served, in many ways, as the beginning of my career as a professional writer, but because in that moment, running the poem back and forth from my seat, I learned something fundamentally true about why being a poet was important to me, and why I would have to engage with this art form for the rest of my life. It left me nowhere to hide. It forced me to confront my guilt, my pain, and all my shortcomings. It demanded that I give an account.

At Union Station I was greeted by handlers, who introduced me to two other performers. It was my first time meeting Mayda Del Valle, the former Nuyorican Grand Slam Champion, whom I recognized from videos online, and a welcome reunion with Jamaica Osorio, whose slam team from Hawaii had won Brave New Voices the year before (and would win it again later that year). The handlers drove us all to the White House in a large black Escalade. We arrived at the front gates, where we met a few of the night's other performers: James Earl Jones, Michael Chabon, Esperanza Spalding, and Lin-Manuel Miranda. After having our IDs checked by agents at the entrance—I don't know for sure that they were Secret Service, but they looked the way Secret Service agents looked on television—we spent an hour or so on a tour of the White House.

After the tour, during rehearsal and a brief sound check, I listened to Jones deliver a monologue from *Othello*, marveled at the speed and grace of Spalding's bass playing, and witnessed Miranda deliver an extended verse in the persona of Alexander Hamilton (this would eventually become *Hamilton*'s opening number). An hour or so later, everyone dressed and went backstage. We recorded audio of James Earl Jones saying "Luke, I am your father." Lin and I started a freestyle cipher that pulled various objects from the rehearsal space into its orbit: "black suit / and a silver tie / hit 'em with the verses that vivify / the room / weary blues take flight from the villain's mind / made it all the way to 1600 Pennsylvania / classic like Othello and Ophelia / Dizzy and Mahalia . . ."

When the event began, the sense of freedom I felt backstage gave way to undeniable anxiety. A sense of heaviness fell over me. Though I had already run the poem hundreds of times, I felt that I was still unprepared for the moment in some deeper sense; an amateur, writing poems in a weathered notebook I had brought from home. And now my mother was seated in the front row, to the direct left of Joe Biden: the youngest of seven children, and the first to go to college. As a girl growing up in the South Bronx, she loved the viola, and even played at Carnegie Hall as a teenager. We never had much in the way of material things. Within the bounds of our household, my mother stressed two matters above all else: faith and the importance of formal education. Nothing will ever be handed to you, she reminded me time and time again. So work as hard as you can, and be ready to stand when your moment arrives.

When my White House moment arrived, I was announced by a voice without a face, soaring through loudspeakers I couldn't see: "And now, the spoken word poet Joshua Brandon Bennett." I ascended the stairs to the stage, barely breathing. I looked out at the crowd, smiled to my mother, and unbuttoned the black suit jacket she had bought for me the week before. I closed my eyes and focused on the image of my sister's face:

Tamara has never listened
to hip-hop
Never danced
to the rhythm of raindrops
or fallen asleep to a chorus of chirping crickets
she has been Deaf
for as long as I have been alive
and ever since the day that I turned five
my father has said:
"Joshua. Nothing is wrong with Tamara.
God just makes
some people different."
And at that moment
those nine letters felt like hammers
swung gracefully by unholy hands
to shatter my stained-glass innocence
into shards that could never be pieced back together
or do anything more
than sever the ties between my sister and I . . .

I still remember her twentieth birthday
readily recall my awestruck eleven-year-old eyes
as I watched Deaf men and women of all ages
dance in unison to the vibrations
of speakers booming so loud
that I imagined angels chastising us
for disturbing their worship
with such beautiful blasphemy.
Until you have seen

a Deaf girl dance
you know nothing of passion.

I recited the entire poem from memory, pulling American Sign Language into my performance as I told the story. After reciting the final line, I took a breath and left the stage. The East Room was a vision. Saul Williams, the actor and poet, and Spike Lee (in a truly unexpected turn) were right there in the audience, cheering me on, alongside college students from Gallaudet (the nation's first university for deaf students), Georgetown, and American University, signing and singing their approval. It was the most important performance of my life to that point.

When it was over, Secret Service agents (I checked to make sure this time) walked the entire group of performers through the front gates. With my mother by my side, I hailed a cab at the corner of Pennsylvania Avenue. Lying in bed, I felt a sudden wave of disappointment. I had loved to write, to perform, for as long as I could remember, and never imagined those passions leading me toward anything like this; an occasion that felt like it was about something much larger than me as an individual poet. I was there—alongside Mayda and Jamaica and Lin and James and Esperanza and others— to represent the art forms we had committed our lives to. What could I ever accomplish that would top an audience with world leaders and standard bearers in my chosen field? I had gotten the chance of a lifetime. What would come next? These were questions that would take me years to answer on terms that felt sufficient. But just for a moment, that night, the stress gave way to a kind of relief. The moment hadn't been too big for me. With the people I loved most at my side, I shook off the weight of my fear. And flew.

*

All the first poets I heard were preachers, but none was more influential than Dr. Millicent Hunter, pastor of a North Philadelphia church called the Baptist Worship Center. The building itself, built to hold hundreds, was a sanctuary and office space converted from a chain supermarket megastore by the side of the highway, with white walls, a triumphant golden cross, and bright amethyst carpeting. Every Sunday, I watched a constellation of strangers weeping, shouting, and sprinting down the aisles of the church as the pastor preached. Two decades before I came to identify as a writer in any meaningful sense, I learned a lesson in that sanctuary I would never forget: what you say, and how you say it, means everything. Truth is embedded in the telling. Indeed, the telling is another kind of truth altogether.

My mother and I would drive for two hours on Sundays to hear Dr. Hunter speak. Just us two, a mother and her strange, untamable boy, her glove box full of gospel CDs and freshly printed MapQuest directions, a pair of McDonald's breakfast sandwiches warming the console between the seats. What I remember most clearly about Dr. Hunter's sermons is the tempo, the precision of the pace, the rise and fall of the writing to match the ebb and flow of emotion in the crowd: people crying, dancing in place, almost immovable once the spirit caught hold of them. My sense, even then, was that Dr. Hunter was not just a masterful communicator all on her own, but a *conduit*, a messenger through whom a power beyond our mortal eyes could enter the space. And the sermon, the epic poetry of that space echoed forth from the pulpit, was the vehicle. The sermon was where language and divine power united. It was the instrument used by the prophet to take us higher.

In those moments, my experience of the black church taught me what it would mean to *write for the people*, for an audience with dreams, and needs, and visions of the future more expansive than I could easily imagine, but that I must nonetheless aim for if I was to be worthy of the gift I wasn't yet sure I had but already aspired toward. The stakes of that writing were life and death. Love and loss. Eternity.

Spoken word is the Western world's oldest form of literary expression. The epic poems we are taught in school today— the *Odyssey*, the *Iliad*, and the like—were not originally conceived as written texts but rather as elaborate performances, as public recitation for crowds of everyday people. Spoken word, in this sense, is where poetry as we know it begins. Oral performance precedes written mastery.

This dynamic is likewise reflected in the roots of spoken-word poetry in the United States: a group of friends assembled in a room, or a bar, or a basement, with nowhere else to go, creating a forum and a form through which they and other marginalized artists could speak their truth to power. No matter how you looked, how you sounded, or where you were born, if you had a story to tell, and were willing to tell it like it mattered, there was space for you. This is still true of spoken word today, an international community that stretches from Denver, Colorado, to Delhi, India, and encompasses middle school, high school, and college programs, as well as the individual efforts of academics, activists, and community organizers around the globe. In the international spoken-word community, there is enough room for each and every one of us—room to share, to make mistakes, and to imagine ourselves anew.

Across the US, high-school curricula have dedicated entire sections of their syllabi to spoken-word poetry. Several award-winning motion pictures (*SlamNation, Slam, Blindspotting*) and televised documentaries (HBO's *Brave New Voices,* ESPN's *One Night in Vegas*) have featured spoken word either as subject matter or as a primary narrative device. Every year, thousands of young people gather in any one of a set of rotating host cities for the largest poetry slam for young people anywhere in the world: the Brave New Voices International Youth Poetry Festival. And there are many more such competitions in the US on an annual basis: the Women of the World Poetry Slam, the National Poetry Slam, and the College Unions Poetry Slam Invitational, just to name a few. According to Poetry Slam, Inc., there are currently over a hundred registered poetry slam venues in the United States. One of the most recent College Unions Poetry Slam Invitationals featured sixty-five teams. In major cities such as Philadelphia, organizations like the Philly Slam League help organize competitive poetry slams for high schools across the city.

Simply put, spoken word is the best possible rejoinder to anyone claiming that poetry in this country is dead or not relevant to younger generations. A search for the term "poetry slam" on YouTube yields videos with tens of millions of views each, and comment sections overflowing with gratitude, rage, and everything in between. Spoken word has always been a haven for oppressed peoples; from its infancy in the 1960s to its current heyday, the most prominent figures in the modern spoken-word movement have been black and brown poets, many of whom have a strong political bent to their writing. Think of luminaries from the 1960s and '70s such as Amiri Baraka (poet, playwright, and founding member of the Black Arts Movement), Sonia Sanchez (recent winner of the Wallace Stevens Award for lifetime achievement from the Academy of American Poets), and Nikki Giovanni (civil rights activist, best-selling recording artist, and recently retired professor of English at Virginia Tech). Any number of contemporary hip-hop artists, actors, comedians, and authors have deep connections to this tradition: Dave Chappelle, Common, Jill Scott—the list is expansive and covers not only various genres but several generations of artists. The history of spoken word is American history: a story about race, music, and the pursuit of human dignity.

Indeed, despite spoken word's long-standing influence as an American subculture, there is no book that captures its true impact on the twentieth and twenty-first centuries. This book is an attempt, on one hand, to fill a gap in our collective memory, and illuminate the breadth of its impact. It will do so by both amplifying the voices of some of the most prominent poets in the spoken-word genre, and by evoking the spaces, moments, and scenes where the energy of this art form radiated out most widely to the culture at large. Alongside this act of historical reclamation, my aim herein is also to provide an insider's perspective on the culture that raised me. I'll shine a

light on the poetry slams, open mics, and street-corner per-
formances that shaped my life and my voice as a teenager,
and helped me grow into someone who teaches poetry for a
living—though I'm less concerned with the campuses where
I went to school, and now serve as faculty, than with the
community centers, churches, and local performance venues
where spoken word has always flourished.

This book will weave together narratives of the men and
women who brought spoken word into each of these spaces
and helped create a global literary movement from what was
happening in their living rooms and neighborhood bars.
This book will tell the tale of spoken-word poetry's rise from
local pastime to global phenomenon. It will paint a picture
of where we have been, how we got here, and where we are
going next if we dare to dream.

Throughout the book, spoken word will be defined as
an art form where written verse is crafted expressly with the
intention of being performed for an audience. Though these
poems are often also memorized, what is critically important
for the writers and performers profiled in this book is the
act of performance itself, even if the words are read aloud
rather than recited from memory. This central, defining char-
acteristic of spoken word—that work is written to be read
aloud, rather than to exist primarily on the page—is, I think,
a critical component of its popularity. At its heart, spoken
word is a social form. It demands engagement and requires
an audience of listeners in order to function. The story of the
past half-century of spoken word in the United States is one
of struggle, but also of persistance and indomitable joy. I'll
contend that several small, devoted collectives helped estab-

lish one of the most influential literary movements of our time: one that has had an indelible influence on any number of writers, actors, musicians, and everyday people across the planet who might not make art at all anymore, professionally or otherwise, but nonetheless performed at an open mic in high school or college, or attended a slam in adulthood, or came across a viral YouTube video while scrolling through their timeline and found themselves moved by a stranger's narration of their interior world.

It bears mentioning here, as well, that there are a number of slam competitions, permutations of the original slam format, and iterations of the spoken word that are not directly covered in this work but that are featured within the larger scholarship on oral poetry and performance. These include but are not limited to the Glam Slam at the Nuyorican Poets Cafe, the ASL slam, and the Southern Fried Poetry Slam. Though these electric expressions of the form are not the explicit focus of this study, they nonetheless demand our attention, and are sterling representatives of the power and aesthetic breadth of the genre.[*]

The sheer energy and expansive reach of this movement is in no small part the product of the tireless work of artists who dared to love those who were deemed unworthy of it. In this sense, *Spoken Word* is a love story of sorts. In bringing to life the founders of the Nuyorican Poets Cafe, the earliest days of poetry slam as an art form, and the current wave of writers who came to prominence as spoken-word poets but are

---

[*] For more on the Glam Slam in particular, see Karen Jaime, *The Queer Nuyorican: Racialized Sexualities and Aesthetics in Loisaida* (NYU Press, 2021).

now directors, actors, musicians, academics, organizers, and literary giants in their own right, I will focus on the spaces that brought these people together. Though competition—through the poetry slam format—helped to spread the art form and its practice widely, I believe that *camaraderie*, rather than *competition as an end unto itself*, is the most useful frame through which to interpret the history of spoken word. Rather than emphasizing the arguments that helped define the landscape of spoken word in its early days, or simply recounting a list of the people who helped spread the art form across the world, I will focus on the relationship between individual brilliance and collective striving that defined this movement. By highlighting the work of young writers from the past as well as those currently performing spoken word in classrooms the world over, I hope to illustrate just how much ground we have covered in the past fifty years—how far we have come, from living rooms full of friends to packed venues the world over—and just how high we can reach.

I have lived out every part of the story I hope to tell in this book. I have recited my work at poetry slams in London taverns, middle-school cafeterias in the South Bronx, at sold-out venues around the world—Madison Square Garden, the Shrine Auditorium, the Kennedy Center, the Sundance Institute, the Elizabeth Sneddon Theatre in South Africa—and at the White House. My entire life has been this complex balancing act, this delicate dance between performance and observation, spotlight and archive.

I cannot imagine my path to life as a professor, or the transformative experiences I have had along the way, without the gift of spoken word and the countless teachers, coaches, and loved ones who helped me hone my relationship to the craft. They were the ones who, year in and year out, in moments of both tragedy and triumph, reminded me that I could always go back to the page, to the music in my mind, to find language that not only communicated my individual struggle, but also might allow me to connect that struggle to that of other human beings across space and time. Part of my aim here, in chronicling the evolution and widespread influence of this art form, is to pay something toward that tremendous debt. So rather than a definitive, comprehensive account, the final word on the matter, this book is meant to be an invitation: one point in a much larger constellation of stories about what the vibrant, living art of the spoken word means to those who have made, and continue to make, a home there.

Book 1:
The Nuyoricans

I came from a family where culture prevailed. My folks gave me a love of culture. So there is nothing surprising about Shakespeare being in my life. It would be surprising if he weren't. I work for him and he works for me. He wanted to have a place to tell the story of England; so I wanted to have a place in which to tell the story of the Lower East Side.

—Miguel Algarín

Well, I guess I started stealing when I was eight. Stealing bread for my baby sister and brother. And other times you walk into the supermarket and just eat the food right out of the aisles, and not even pay. We'd walk right outside, you know? Now when you think about Latin writers, you probably think about Señor Márquez, Neruda, Cortázar—the magic realism. Not here, not this. There are no floating butterflies around my head when I walk down Avenue B, you know. This is street reality. This is where we shout it out. Shout it out.

—Miguel Piñero

On a Friday night in November of 2006, my senior year in high school, I put on a royal-blue T-shirt emblazoned with Bob Marley's face, and a pair of red-and-white Nikes I'd purchased with my Foot Locker employee discount.* I boarded the 1 train from 242nd Street after taking the BX9 bus from my childhood home, heading south for Manhattan, to a placed called the Nuyorican Poets Cafe. Earlier that fall, I qualified for my first city-wide youth poetry slam, which was to be held at the famous East Village bar and global center for spoken word: the most famous poetry slam venue in the world. The only other time I had been to the Village was to purchase my first album, Juelz Santana's *From Me to U*, from a record shop not too far from the Cafe. I would keep the record as contraband that year—no hip-hop allowed in the house—letting its sharp cadences and outlandish tales of uptown bravado color the raps I recited to myself in the still moments between studying for English class and writing for the stage, which by November had already become my second job, alongside the gig at Foot Locker. The walk from the D train to the Cafe was an education. All the elements of my surroundings were turned up to ten: each radiant color

---

* Working at this specific Foot Locker, located in the Westchester mall, was my first job. It was also my first training ground as a poet. Whenever I wasn't at school or church, I spent most of my time there, practicing poems in the back room as I searched for Jordans and New Balance running shoes. All those hours milling about the store gave me time to think, and to compose the lines I thought would resonate most powerfully with an audience of strangers.

and irrepressible sound. Bass blasting from the windows of cars, dollar pizza shops packed from wall to wall, rows of sunglasses stacked higher than any passerby. When you got to the part of Avenue C where the Cafe lives, you knew it immediately by the line that stretched all the way down the block (whether we're talking Wednesday or Friday, it made no difference, I would soon learn), the large black awning and booth that led to the door, and the mural on the wall depicting the famed Nuyorican poet Pedro Pietri. Pietri was sketched in blue and black and surrounded by red bricks on all sides. The mural also featured five faceless figures in hats and trench coats, as if a collective composed entirely of detectives who also happened to be ghosts.

It took about twenty minutes to get to the front of the line, at which point I paid the entrance fee and stepped inside the venue. The first thing I saw was the blast of Technicolor: red and blue and bright yellow where the stage lights hit the back of the room. All the chairs in the venue were aimed toward the back of the space, where there was a bright vermilion rug onstage, and a wireless microphone in a metal stand on top of that. There were paintings all over the walls, and a DJ in the back spinning records in and out of one another at warp speed. The room was bristling, alive.

On the night of that first slam, my big sister, Latoya, had just returned home from her senior year of college. She came all the way down from Yonkers to the Lower East Side to see me perform. The host that night was a poet and emcee named Jive Poetic, and the place was packed. As is custom, the DJ played Bell Biv DeVoe's timeless hit "Poison" right after the judges were chosen and right before the sacrificial poet touched the stage. Thankfully, I didn't draw the first slot during this particular slam. Generally speaking, no one wants to go first. When that happens, you have to set the tone for the night, and have no idea what kind of work your competitors will bring to the table. Whether you opt for a funny poem or something a bit more politically charged becomes a gut decision, instead of a strategic choice based on audience reaction and the poet who performs right before you. It's a tough spot to be in.

Ten teenagers signed up for that night's competition and discerning an early favorite would have been difficult amid such a large field. I did my best to stand out. As a friend's former mentor used to say, "Your poem starts before you touch the stage"—by which she meant that the process of communicating who you are, what you are about, begins the moment the audience first sees you, before you have even opened your mouth. It may have been my first time performing at the Nuyorican, but I was familiar with the lore. I knew that when the poetry resonated, it got wild in there: people yelling, banging on tables, laughing so loudly that you could barely hear the poet. Likewise, you could just as easily tell when the crowd wasn't into it, and that was my worst fear— not rejection so much as indifference. The point of slam is not simply to be heard. You want to be engaged, encountered, unforgettable.

The poem I performed that night was the first one I had ever written for the stage: "The Talented Tenth." As its title suggests, it was a meditation on W. E. B. Du Bois's theory of racial uplift.* The ideas that would eventually become "Talented Tenth" were shaped during the two-hour commute from my parents' house to my private high school in Rye, and then back again each day. For all four years of high school, I would wake up at five a.m. and speed down the block with my laptop and books in my backpack while just about everyone else in the neighborhood, my family included, was still asleep. On those walks, I would think at length about what it meant to have been selected for this opportunity. I knew that my friends, family, and classmates from childhood all would have benefited greatly from the sort of educational resources I now had access to. Until I discovered slam, I was never able to put that feeling into words, and wrestle with what it meant to me, and for how I should live my life. Though I was exposed to poetry at home—Toya kept a copy of Maya Angelou's "Phenomenal Woman" taped to her bedroom door—the spoken word poets who entered my life my senior year, once I started going to slams, had an energy to their work that felt altogether new. For one thing, the vast majority of the poets I met around that time were my age. They used profanity unabashedly (to my mother's chagrin), they talked about teenage angst, structural inequality, and global revolution in evocative ways, often addressing all these subjects in the span of a single poem. I knew from the very beginning that I had found my people—and my calling.

Jive Poetic called out my name, and I walked up to the

---

* It bears mentioning here that Du Bois would eventually retract this theory publicly, citing its various limitations as a vision for social justice and collective liberation.

microphone to mild applause and the discernible voice of
my sister yelling "Let's go, Josh!" from the front row. I took
a moment to survey the crowd, closed my eyes, and tried to
reimagine the scenes that brought me to this moment. The
venue was packed to the brim that night. The stage lights
shone so brightly I could barely see beyond the front row.
The poem began:

I am a member of the Talented Tenth
W. E. B. Du Bois's theory in the flesh
The cream of the crop
the best of the best
or at least that's what I'm told
by my standardized tests . . .

The poem clocked in at a little under three minutes,
in accordance with the slam rules I had memorized well
in advance. It reckoned with my experience of double-
consciousness not only as someone who is both black and
American—what Du Bois describes as "two warring ideals
in one dark body"—but as a child of working people who
attended an elite, predominately white high school. It then
moved to a much larger narrative about racial discrimination
and injustice, detailing the history of segregation, lynching,
and structural poverty that I had learned from my parents
over the years. Like so many spoken-word performances,
"Talented Tenth" was a combination of autobiography and
social critique. It was my attempt to hold a mirror up to
myself and my surroundings at the same time, to invite every-
one within earshot to hear my story and to see a piece of

themselves in it. The performance went over well, and I was awarded a near-perfect score by the judges. Ultimately, I was selected as one of the winners of that night's slam who would go on to compete in the semifinal phase of the citywide youth poetry slam competition. After the bout, Latoya took me out to Wendy's to celebrate. It was truly a banner night.

Sitting at the bar that evening was a man named Miguel Algarín. I had never met him, or even heard of him, before that night's slam. When I returned to the scene in earnest during the summers after my freshman, sophomore, and junior years of college, Miguel remembered me, and would say so. He never offered advice, or feedback on individual poems, or anything like that. The point, I think, was simply to clarify that the work had resonated with him. It would take me almost a decade of study after those first encounters with Algarín to begin to understand his contribution to the art form I was every day growing to love and setting out to transform in my own way. Without my knowing it, his dreams had been the foundation for my own.

Miguel passed away on November 30, 2020, at the age of seventy-nine. The Nuyorican Poets Cafe was his creation, and he handed it down, along with other elders who were his friends and colleagues, many of them literary giants who became ancestors too soon, and some who walk among us even still. My performance in that room, standing in the building their poems helped to create from the ground up, was one of my points of origin as a poet. And not only for me, but for hundreds of writers over the past fifty years who have come through the doors of the Nuyorican—whether in its earliest form, in Miguel's living room, or at the Sunshine

Tavern, or in the Alphabet City venue where it currently resides—in search of a haven, or fame, or a tradition they could call their own. A place you can stumble into and get lost for hours in the confessions of strangers. An encounter with a living history you'll never forget.

The Living Room

The voices you hear are coming from the first floor of a Lower East Side apartment building, the color of sandstone, on Sixth Street. The calendar above the clock reads May 1973. If you look through the window to the outside world, you can barely make out bags of trash and a pair of trees just across the street, their finer details blurred at this point in the evening. But you can still see the cavalcade of everyday people on the street, carrying their bags from the local bodegas and family-owned pizzerias that feed the block. Back inside, the place is packed. It is usually filled to capacity even on weekday nights, when the writers begin arriving in the early evening and stay until well after night has cast its long black cloak over the proceedings. The twenty or so regulars sit on the couch, on the floor, and on the extra one or two chairs that are always there, unfolded in expectation of the evening's labor. Those gathered—luminaries like Ntozake Shange, Lucky CienFuegos, Sandra Maria Esteves—read, share lines, and try out new material. They edit one another in real time. They bring their full selves to the process of building this new work in ensemble.

The apartment belongs to a Rutgers professor of English and Puerto Rican studies named Miguel Algarín. He is thirty-two years old. Already, he is a renaissance man like few others. Raised in Santurce, Puerto Rico, until the age of nine, Algarín came to New York City with his family on July 13, 1951, and remained there for his entire life. They initially went to live with his aunt, Carmen Ana Figueras—a singer, entrepreneur, and published poet—on 121st Street and Pleasant Avenue. His mother, Maria Socorro Algarín, was also a writer, and a young Miguel was seen to have inherited his literary gifts from her. She would eventually publish a collection of poems, *Lluvias de otoño* (which translates to English as *Autumn Showers*), after his first book was published.

Young Algarín was a voracious reader, and he acted in school plays. An academically gifted student from an early age, he would go on to study at the University of Wisconsin–Madison, at Penn State, and finally at Rutgers University, where he earned a PhD in comparative literature. For his poetry and prose, Algarín would eventually earn an Obie, a Bessie, and three American Book Awards. His unique combination of academic training and upbringing made him an ideal leader for the original, core group of Nuyorican Poets. He had the access, resources, and expertise needed to bridge the diverse community he had grown up in and the literary world that had ignored it for so long. In opening his apartment to the public, and eventually putting up his own money to open the Nuyorican, Algarín provided a model of literary citizenship that is truly rare. Though it would have been much easier, perhaps, to simply serve as a liaison between his homegrown literary community and the ivory tower, he chose instead to blur that distinction altogether; to create a new, alternative space where historically marginalized voices could flourish on their own terms once they arrived in Loisaida. Many of the people walking by outside, of course, would describe this part of Manhattan with less sonorous, more common monikers: the Lower East Side, Alphabet City, Greenwich Village, or simply *Downtown*. The list of names was as varied as the vibrant colors of flags you would see in the windowsills of Loisaida back then.

Years before I or any other young poet ever stepped inside what would become the Nuyo's headquarters in this neighborhood, it was a living room filled with poets from across the city, sharing their work freely. The Cafe's current website lists the founding poets, twenty names, including those of Diane Burns (a Native American poet who was invited by the Sandinista government to read her work in Nicaragua in the early 1970s), Lucky CienFuegos (poet, activist, and playwright who was featured extensively in the first-ever *New York Times* article about the Nuyorican), and Ntozake Shange (award-winning author and leading light of second-wave black feminism).

Twenty founders: Miguel Algarín, Richard August, Shorty Bon Bon, Jorge Brandon, Diane Burns, Americo Casiano, Lucky CienFuegos, Sandra Maria Esteves, Eddie Figueroa, Meredith Genin (aka Belle Starr), Lois Elaine Griffith, Tato Laviera, Miguel Loperena, Jesús Papoleto Meléndez, Jose Parreño, Rev. Pedro Pietri, Miguel Piñero, Bimbo Rivas, Raul Santiago Sebazco, and Ntozake Shange. Twenty poets, playwrights, and polymaths.

Some, like Shange, author of the world-famous choreopoem *For Colored Girls Who Have Considered Suicide / When the Rainbow Is Enuf*, would eventually become prominent writers (Shange also staged some of the first performances of

For Colored Girls at the Nuyorican). But nearly all of these names have been left out of the way we often narrate the history of spoken word. And though the poets mentioned above are counted among the official founders, one imagines that there were many other writers, participants, and passers-through who helped make the Nuyorican what it was then, in its early years, and what it is today. The founding poets had any number of different styles and approaches to their craft. There was no single aesthetic that brought them together. The group was formed by a sense of shared purpose and further unified by an aloneness imposed from outside, a rejection on the basis of their lived identities and on the highly politicized content of their work. Within that space, they found a way to be alone together, and to hold one another up in a world that did not understand them.

"Nuyorican" is a term with a complex history. For some, it is little more than casual shorthand: "New York Puerto Rican" honed into a four-syllable identity. For others, its immediate association is with the Cafe.* In a 1990 *Newsday* interview, Miguel Algarín offers an origin story for his specific use of the term:

> Miguel Piñero . . . and myself took a trip to Puerto Rico to do [poetry] readings. As we were walking in the air-port, we saw people were looking at us. Mikey had an enormous Afro. We were wearing those platform shoes people wore in the 70s. We'd been speaking English to

* Here I'm thinking specifically about Bob Holman's controversial claim in *The New York Times* that "we are all Nuyorican," which was rebuffed by Pedro Pietri.

each other, and we kept hearing: "Look at the Nuyo-
ricans." It was a put-down. It caught us by total sur-
prise. When we came back here, we needed a title for
the anthology of poetry by Puerto Ricans in New York
that we'd put together. We decided to call it Nuyorican
Poetry, to turn the put-down around.[1]

Alongside Algarín's account, it's important to consider the
ways that the broader Nuyorican movement was shaped by
the children of Puerto Rican migrants in the 1940s and '50s
who arrived in New York in the wake of Operation Bootstrap,
a stimulus program inaugurated in 1947 by Luis Muñoz
Marín, who became governor of Puerto Rico in 1949 and
held the post for sixteen years. Operation Bootstrap offered
tax incentives to companies throughout North America to
develop manufacturing plants on the island, which ulti-
mately transformed the Puerto Rican economy, and directly
impacted the fortunes of thousands of its residents who were
pushed to seek employment in the States, and especially in
New York City.

The generation of Nuyorican activists, intellectuals, art-
ists, and writers that was born out of this historical moment
helped foment nothing short of a cultural revolution that was
anticolonial in nature, global in its scope, and ultimately pro-
duced a Nuyorican sound, a Nuyorican aesthetic, that is still
with us today, transferred through generations of avant-garde
performance and public action. This period was known as
El Nuevo Despertar, or the New Awakening. In its commit-
ments to social justice, and the range of genres through which
those commitments might be enacted and explored—not

only poetry, but music and live theater—the Nuyorican Poets Cafe stood, even in its earliest instantiations, as an exemplary institution of this moment in time. Nuyorican poets were not only consummate performers. They participated in civil rights struggle, antiwar protests, and local initiatives to rehabilitate various parts of the city destroyed by active neglect. They performed in the New York Shakespeare Festival. They gathered in private and in public and declaimed the truths of their beloved communities.

A striking example of this collision of performance and radical politics, from the living-room years, pre-Nuyo as such, is captured in the 1971 film *El Pueblo Se Levanta* (The People Are Rising), which documents the December 28, 1969, takeover of the 1st Spanish United Methodist Church in East Harlem by the Young Lords Party. This was a direct response to a physical assault on members of the YLP by several undercover police officers, which took place after an attempt to address the congregation about their new community-centered project: a free-breakfast program for neighborhood residents. Two weeks after several of the Young Lords were not only beaten but arrested, the eleven-day occupation of the church, which they renamed La Iglesia del Pueblo—the People's Church— began. During the protest, the Young Lords combined a series of community initiatives—a daycare center, clothing drives, and a version of the free-breakfast program they had proposed earlier—with regular performances. One of the featured performers was none other than foundational Nuyorican poet Pedro Pietri, who debuted his classic poem "Puerto Rican Obituary" within the space. Its closing stanza looked like this:

Juan
Miguel
Milagros
Olga
Manuel
will right now be doing their own thing
where beautiful people sing
and dance and work together
where the wind is a stranger
to miserable weather conditions
where you do not need a dictionary
to communicate with your people
Aqui
Se Habla Espanol
all the time
Aqui you salute your flag first
Aqui there are no dial soap commercials
Aqui everybody smells good
Aqui tv dinners do not have a future
Aqui the men and women admire desire
and never get tired of each other
Aqui Que Pasa Power is what's happening
Aqui to be called negrito
means to be called LOVE[2]

In 1972, three years after that Pietri performed this poem,
Miguel Algarín led a workshop called El Puerto Rican Play-
wrights'/Actors' Workshop at 4 Astor Place, a working space
they were offered by the Public Theater's Joseph Papp. In

collaboration with the theater artist Raymond Barry as well as a group of kung fu instructors he brought in to help the participants embody their work more fully—these martial-arts classes were serious business and lasted for two hours—Algarín worked with a group of playwrights to cultivate a set of original works. When EPRP/AW was forced to leave its space downtown due to budget cuts, Papp invited Miguel Piñero—who had just finished serving a sentence at Sing Sing prison—to a workshop session. There he met Algarín, and the two began a friendship that would last the rest of their lives.

Before there was a brick-and-mortar café, the Nuyorican poets could be found speaking back to the harsh conditions of the world around them with language born directly from the cauldron of that experience. As Algarín wrote in *Nuyorican Poetry: An Anthology of Puerto Rican Words and Feelings*, which he coedited with Piñero: "The experience of Puerto Ricans on the streets of New York has caused a new language to grow: Nuyorican. Nuyoricans are a special experience in the immigration history of the city of New York. We come to the city as citizens and retain the use of Spanish and include English. . . . The interchange between both yields new verbal possibilities, new images to deal with the stresses of living on tar and cement."[3] For Algarín, then, Nuyorican was not only an identity marker but a *language*, an *experience*, fecund earth from which new image systems and political possibilities might emerge. Nuyorican, from this vantage, is inextricable from a certain way of talking about what it means to build, and mourn, and live together—to survive here in a strange land bent on our destruction. It is a bridge and a bunker. A balm in the wound of an ongoing struggle.

Miguel Algarín's living room was the hotspot for these windswept romantics—for the refugees, first movers, and unrepentant freedom fighters, men and women squarely positioned both in the prime of their lives and at the edge of the social safety net. How does one describe what Algarín and company set out to achieve during nights spent in that room for two years straight, working relentlessly, seriously, as the sounds of the time echoed through the landscape just beyond the glass? One might be tempted in the present day to think of Algarín's gatherings simply as a kind of writing retreat, or else a workshop for the black and brown avant-garde of the early 1970s. But look again: there is little in the way of stringent routine here; the ceremony begins when the people arrive and ends when they depart. This was a key ingredient in what would become the worldwide movement of spoken word: it happened in a room where people gathered to share in a spirit of urgency. It was about both a set of generative social interactions and a serious commitment to producing new work together. One of the earliest participants in the Nuyo living-room sessions, Pedro Pietri, phrased it this way: "All these poets would congregate there . . . Jesús Papoleto Meléndez, Lucky CienFuegos, Bimbo Rivas, Shorty Bon Bon, my brother, Dr. Willie [Pietri]. We used to stay in [Algarín's] living room and recite poetry. We felt really good about it because at the time we didn't have space, we didn't have an audience, we were all we had. It was exciting in the beginning; we were young, struggling artists. It was like

Magic; everything was so important."[4] Even in the absence of an audience, then, the earliest Nuyorican poets maintained a commitment to one another, and to the most radical vision of what their gathering might mean to the outside world. But once the weekend is over, Miguel must return to his day job.

I learn about Miguel's work as a scholar and teacher primarily through my time spent at the Center for Puerto Rican Studies at Hunter College, poring through the archives. There are ten boxes or so of material on his life and legacy there, each containing its own, unique treasures. I begin with his C.V., in part to piece together a fuller picture of Miguel Algarín the educator, rather than solely the poet, editor, or entrepreneur, as he is perhaps best known. It shows that for forty-one years, between 1965 and 2006, Algarín taught in the English department at Rutgers University, first as an instructor (until 1972), then as an assistant professor (1972–1977), before eventually earning tenure in 1977 and being promoted to the rank of associate professor. From 1965 to 1967, Algarín was also a lecturer in English composition and literature at Brooklyn College. I try to imagine the ornate structure of his work life during this period: teaching at two institutions while writing poems and plays, hosting sessions in his living room, and eventually founding the Nuyorican Poets Cafe only a short walk away from his front door.

The Brooklyn that Algarín knew and explored during this period in his life was on the cusp of one of the more significant, long-standing demographic shifts in the history of the borough. In the early 1980s, the neighborhood where Brooklyn College is located, Flatbush, would become home to a wave of immigrant families from across the world. The

Joseph Papp presents

POETS OF THE CITY

Associate Producer Bernard Gersten

SEVEN ROOSTERS AND THREE DRUNKEN POETS

POETS

Pedro Juan Pietri
Jesus Papoleto Melendez
Dr. Willie Pietri

INTERMISSION

THE NUYORICAN POETS

Directed by Miguel Algarín
Mural of Chango by Tony Rivera
Dancer's Costumes by Mario Garcia and Thea Martinez
Choreographed by Thea Martinez

POETS

Miguel Algarín
Miguel Piñero*
Lucky CienFuegos
Sandra María Esteves

MUSICIANS

Milton Cardona	Conga
Willie García	Singer
Frankie Rodriguez	Conga
Gene Golden	Conga
Joe Santiago	Bass
Eddie Martinez	Piano
Henry Gonzalez	Saxophone
Charlie Santiago	Bongos and Timbales

DANCERS

Thea Martinez
Sherrell A. Mash
Amneris Rodriguez

LADY IN RED

Mimi Marrero

Stage Manager - Richard August

* Equity member appearing through the courtesy of Actor's Equity
Association.

largest share of these new Brooklynites would arrive from the then Soviet Union, but a substantial number of folks also arrived from Jamaica, Ireland, Guyana, Mexico, and Haiti, from Poland and Italy and Greece, Latvia and Lithuania, Pakistan and Iran, China and Bangladesh. Over the course of a decade, Flatbush would become one of the most diverse neighborhoods in the United States.

This was the environment that shaped a young Miguel Algarín, fresh out of graduate school at Rutgers, still finding his legs as a scholar and teacher, still developing the sensibility that eventually led him to write that "the poet is responsible for inventing the newness. The newness needs words, words never heard before or used before. The poet has to invent a new language, a new tradition of communication."[5] Taken away for hours by necessity from the familiar beauty of Loisaida, he was able to discover himself anew in this increasingly diverse section of Brooklyn. At the collision point of an abundance of new languages, new traditions and cultural practices, the early-thirtysomething professor continued to further develop his own style, working full-time as both an educator and an organizer of the increasingly packed performance sessions in his living room back home on the Lower East Side.

On these rides out from lower Manhattan, we can imagine Algarín reworking lecture notes on a yellow pad, running the lines back and forth through his mind. Today, he is preparing for the morning section of his course on the life and works of William Shakespeare. The midterm is coming up in two weeks, and he wants to land his lecture on *Rich-*

ard II smoothly. He's practicing hand motions, pauses, with the pencil behind his ear as the tunnel blurs on either side of the subway car, he and an unwieldy ensemble of strangers all huddled inside of its steel body daydreaming, making plans for lunch, regretting something left unsaid earlier that morning. Perhaps he should add a few more lines about the symbolic importance, in the present day, of these lines in act 5, scene 5, a striking reminder of the concerns that brought so many of them into the class at the opening of the semester:

> Thus play I in one person many people,
> And none contented. Sometimes am I king.
> Then treasons make me wish myself a beggar,
> And so I am; then crushing penury
> Persuades me I was better when a king.
> Then am I kinged again, and by and by
> Think that I am unkinged by Bolingbroke,
> And straight am nothing. But whate'er I be,
> Nor I nor any man that but man is
> With nothing shall be pleased till he be eased
> With being nothing.[6]

How to reach such a place, eased with being nothing? And was this sense of things a form of freedom or of bondage for the students he had slowly, day by day, class by class, been growing to love, these poor and working-class young people from across the world, gathered here in a small classroom at the edge of Brooklyn to read Shakespeare? And for what, exactly? For many of the same reasons, he imagined, that he had spent the better part of the past five years in New Jersey studying the Bard: that fundamental human desire to craft worlds out of language. And what's more, the related but distinct pursuit and dream of having others want to live there with you, if for only a moment.

Yes: to build a new world and share it with friends, kin, absolute strangers. This was the dream within the dream of the student of Shakespeare, the young professor writing lines in between the hours he spends penning lectures he hopes will reach the young people under his care. Ishmael Reed would later say of Algarín's writing that "the poetry is as sophisticated as the author, who is capable of leading a theater audience in a discussion of the links between William Shakespeare and Adrienne Kennedy and of ordering in French at a New Orleans restaurant. He is a professor who nevertheless hasn't lost the common touch."[7] The common touch in question was honed in moments like these, dashing through the metropolis, plotting out where in the flow of the lecture he might pause for a moment, to see if there were any questions or else to riff on an interpretation of text that came to him in just that moment of hearing a student read.

While working in his home discipline within the English department at Rutgers, Algarín was also helping to develop an institutional presence in Puerto Rican studies, a more recent disciplinary formation that, not unlike a number of other fields that Sylvia Wynter refers to as "new studies"— Black studies, Chicano studies, women's studies—emerged institutionally in the 1960s as the direct result of widespread student protest on college and university campuses across the

United States.* While at Rutgers, Algarín helped helm one of the central sites of this national movement, one fundamentally committed to the study of Puerto Rico's role in global history. In the introduction to *Nuyorican Poetry: An Anthology of Puerto Rican Words and Feelings*, Algarín makes a version of the case for Nuyorican poetry that gestures toward this new intersection of interests emerging in his life:

> The poems in this anthology document the conditions of survival: many roaches, many busts, many drug poems, many hate poems—many, many poems of complaints. But the complaints are delivered in a new rhythm. It is a bomba rhythm with many changing pitches delivered with a bold stress. The pitches vary, but the stress is always bomba and the vocabulary is English and Spanish mixed into a new language.[8]

And elsewhere:

> The poet blazes a path of fire for the self. He juggles with words. He lives risking each moment. Whatever he does, in every way he moves, he is a prince of the inner-city jungle. He is the philosopher of the sugar cane that grows between the cracks of concrete sidewalks.[9]

This commitment to the interplay of various traditions— especially the Puerto Rican culture he knew intimately from

* See Sylvia Wynter, "No Humans Involved," Forum N.H.I. Knowledge for the 21st Century 1, no. 1 (Fall 1994): 52.

study and experience and the Elizabethan tradition that occupied so much of his energy as a student, educator, and scholar—was a key element of Algarín's teaching. For Algarín, there was no easy division to be drawn between the literature he adored and the life he had lived as a child in the metropolis:

> I obviously don't write like him because you can say that no one knows and understands what Shakespeare knew by intuition, when he lived centuries ago, but I feel comfortable using English because the master of English verse is my friend. When he writes historic plays, he uses rhetoric, he uses the concerns of his day to explain the turbulence that affects people in power. He entertained people with stories from the past. He dared to enter into the human psyche. When I teach *Othello* and I see how he dealt with that character, I can appreciate how he makes evil stand out, how he presents those types of people who are out to destroy another person. In a way, I think Shakespeare was a Nuyorican.[10]

One imagines the hours of practice it took to rework the lecture notes in his mind, hands now occupied, before teaching his undergraduate seminars and larger class meetings; the way he would weave between lecture notes and memorized lines of verse from Shakespeare, Neruda, or Stevens, from Spanish to English to French, from a taut line of argumentation to a joke about the friends he grew up with back in Loisaida. His sartorial style was as vibrant as his lectures: from corduroy blazers and chinos and loafers to colorful sweaters to casual polos and back; from a shorter haircut showing off his curls to a resplendent ink-black Afro, shining like the dark side of the moon. Between chairing Puerto Rican studies and his work in the English department, Algarín was always on the clock. He never stopped moving. During these hard weeks of teaching, planning programming and events, grading papers and quizzes, he would head home to the Lower East Side, where a budding movement marked by his friends and closest collaborators was waiting for him to help open the door.

The sessions in Algarín's living room were some combination of a rent party and a rehearsal for the future world, a space forged squarely at the intersections of not only amateur and expert, poetry and drama, but elite academe and state prison, black feminism and decolonial critique. The living room was a collision point. It was a laboratory where all manner of ideas could be adjudicated, vetted, tested out. The most famous work to come out of these sessions would be read, largely, under the genre headings of theater and spoken word. But such designations on their face do little justice to the formal experimentation and sheer range of what was taking place on those evenings in Algarín's living room. The participants were not merely breaking new ground in forms they already knew and loved, but stretching the boundaries of genre distinction, language, and character. They were explorers, interspersing familiar myths, personal narrative, and cultural histories to craft something new and altogether dynamic.

One poet who was there from the beginning was the Dominican Boricua Nuyorican poet and artist Sandra Maria Esteves, who was born and raised in the Bronx, and knew Algarín from before the Nuyorican Poets Cafe was even built.

Her boyfriend was a student in one of Algarín's Brooklyn College classes, and she sat in on one of them; this was how she first learned about his work. She remembers that the Sixth Street apartment was on the ground floor, and that Miguel had use of the backyard to the building, so sometimes people would hang out there as well. "But it was just an apartment," she told me, expressing the informality of the feeling there. "More than anything, there was a lot of talking going on." On several occasions, Esteves helped Algarín with some work; she was hired to type up some of Miguel Piñero's plays. And before long, she was sharing her own work in his living room, along with the rest of the literary vanguard of her time.

The year was 1973. Esteves had only just begun her journey as a poet, and had no idea of the future that awaited her in the process. Born and raised in the Bronx by a Dominican mother and a Puerto Rican father, she lived in Spanish for most of her life, and taught herself English by listening to the radio and reading newspapers. Between the Spanish-dominant milieu of her home life in the Bronx and her life in a strict English-speaking Catholic boarding school on the Lower East Side, she lived at an intersection of languages that were often positioned as being, necessarily, in conflict. Along with the others in Algarín's living room, Esteves knew she was an artist, one still trying to find her home medium as a Nuyorican cultural renaissance blossomed all around her.

She was already a trained visual artist, studying at the Pratt Institute in Brooklyn, when she discovered her latent talent for writing poems, and in particular her sharp eye for imagery. It was in a sculpture class with the world-renowned Japanese-born American sculptor Toshio Odate that she discovered poetry: Odate had them chiseling wood, a very slow and frustrating process, but one day Esteves went into class and there were sheets of typing paper on the wall arranged into sculptures that were "megalithic in size," she recalls, each with three or four lines of text inscribed onto its surface, citing the example of one that included an image of "a pink ribbon floating in a yellow sky."

This was a piece of visual art, she explains, given its charge by language and the dance between paper and written sign. This experience in Odate's classroom awakened the sense within Esteves that words could do a kind of visual work that was intense and immediate. So her love for poetry began in the sculptor's studio, in an unexpected moment of inspiration that spurred along a new set of everyday artistic practices for her—"messing around with words" and trying to create images on the page that approached the vibrance and clarity of the ones she had been inscribing onto canvas, wood, and stone.

Later that year, a friend of her boyfriend, a writer named Jesús Papoleto Meléndez, came over to her house for dinner. Meléndez had been writing poetry since he was very young, and he had just published a book. She shared some of her work with him at that dinner, and he helped introduce her into the early-seventies poetry scene in New York City that was undergoing a total transformation. "I met everybody," she says. "It was an explosion of words and ideas and poets, and not just the Nuyoricans, but the African American poets, the poets from the Black nationalist movement, and poets like Amiri Baraka and Quincy Troupe. In fact, we used to go to Quincy Troupe's house and read our poems aloud. We'd go around in a circle and read our work." This prepared her for Algarín's living room: "By the time I started hanging out with Algarín in his apartment, I already had a sense of my own voice." Esteves, who would eventually go on to write three books of poetry and record two spoken word albums, *DivaNations* and *Wildflowers*, had started receiving some notoriety, which happened fairly quickly. She attributes this in part to the fact there was now a significant population of Latino students in the local universities who were English speakers and excited to hear voices that reflected some recognizable version of their cultural milieu. "They were looking for someone to address the students, someone who wrote in English, and a friend of a friend of a friend says, 'Oh, I know someone,' and that's how I got invited to these various universities." That kick-started Esteves's public persona, the invitations to read her work—which was new for her, and welcome, because it sometimes came with money, and, she says, "I was also a mother. I had a child at that point. So the door opened and I walked through it."

Those early days in the Nuyorican salon on East Sixth Street were both a productive space of creative collaboration and a battleground. Esteves recalls several poets in the space who were very condescending toward the women in the group, "as though we were not as valid as their voices." She adds, "But I was not confused, and I was not silenced. I spoke my mind. That got me in a lot of trouble with a lot of people." Esteves knew that she had something to say and that her voice should be part of the dialogue, and whether other poets in the salon agreed or not was largely irrelevant to her. Her poems had a place in the world now that would not be denied.

Part of the unique sound and sensibility that Estevez brought with her (one can hear echoes of this in her poem "Autobiography of a Nuyorican," where she writes, "half blue, feet first / she battled into the world") came from the Bronx's salsa scene, which she'd discovered in her home neighborhood in her high school years: "a different kind of church," one in which people were unimpeachably joyous, dancing, immersed in the sounds of Joe Cuba and Joe Bataan, of Celia Cruz and Tito Puente and La Lupe. The sound of the horns and congas would fill the dance hall, and all those assembled would sing in unison, swaying in the dark air as if on cue. For Esteves, the beauty and fervor of the dance hall became a respite. As the Bronx burned all around her, she did her best to maintain a sense of herself: "There was an exodus of everybody, including my mom, and I remember one time I had a dream where I was walking down Longwood Avenue and I was stepping on burnt flesh."

The harrowing dream, for Esteves, represented all the neighborhoods she knew well that were presently being torn apart; how she and her friends were now separated from one another, from their confidantes and loved ones. A few of them started moving out toward the West Bronx, near the Grand Concourse area, and the fires began happening there, too. It felt as if the flames were following them, from one part of the borough to another. Eventually, a new sound rose from the wreckage: hip-hop was coming into being. From where Esteves lived, on Morris Avenue and 176th Street, she could see from her window the train cars passing in the distance, adorned, even on the inside, with aerosol art. Everything was tagged. You couldn't escape the sense of that vibrant sound shifting the landscape.

Esteves observed these changes taking place in the Bronx while still spending much of her time in Brooklyn and the Lower East Side, where a different, though related, arts scene was taking hold. "Around the corner from the Nuyorican was the New Rican Village, another cultural center where a lot of folks hung out. That was directed by Eddie Figueroa, a theater person. . . . I met Jerry González and Andy González and a lot of the [folks] from Conjunto Libre, and they started jamming there on Thursdays. . . . I also met Pedro Pietri there; his sister became the administrator of the café. In fact, Eddie Figueroa produced a number of Pedro's plays at the New Rican Village."

Along with the New Rican Village, Esteves remembers Miriam Colón's Puerto Rican Traveling Theater, and the Taller Boricua (which is still around, by the way, on 106th Street and Lexington), and the Museo del Barrio. All these spaces were part of the scene in which the Nuyorican Poets Cafe developed; it was not the only place, Esteves says, in which the difficult miracle of black poetry and the unimpeachable power of the Nuyorican sound were being formed at this time. There was an entire network of institutions, formal and informal, that served as a bedrock for the worldshifting literature being produced in this moment. "Some people say it was a cultural renaissance, and maybe it was," she tells me. "I think it was the blossoming of the Puerto Ricans in New York who spoke English."

Within two years of the first readings in Algarín's living room, in 1975, the number of poets attending grew too large for his modest apartment on East Sixth Street. Eager to keep the creative momentum going, he began renting a local pub across the street, the Sunshine Tavern, for one night every week, as the venue for gatherings of around fifty people. The pub was small, and dimly lit, and ideal for the kind of cutting-edge work that the Nuyorican poets were putting out in the world. This new home was the first public forum for the salons that had taken place in the apartment for over a year, and it allowed the original group to continue to meet, write, and perform together. Thanks in no small part to Algarín's ingenuity, the collective now had far more room to work and started to gain a significant audience. College students, literary critics, and organizers packed the Sunshine from wall to wall. Onlookers came from every borough to experience the magic the poets created on a weekly basis. When audiences eventually ballooned beyond the Sunshine Tavern's capacity, Algarín made the decision to find a new venue. In 1978, the Nuyorican Poets Cafe found a home at 236 East Third Street. That same year, Algarín applied for federal grants to renovate the building, and received $350,000 in funding from the New York City Department of Cultural Affairs. During the process of that renovation, serious structural damage was discovered within the building. In 1982, the Nuyorican was forced to close its doors, and it remained shuttered for seven years. In 1989, the Nuyorican reopened. The venue returned to prominence amid a spoken-word renaissance by then taking place across the country.

Even in its earliest days, it was clear that this group of writers had created a sound, a scene, that reflected the best of the art form while also offering a window into what the future might hold. The roots of what Esteves had seen uptown—of what would eventually become hip-hop culture—were on vivid display in the earliest performances at the Nuyorican. It was all there: the political consciousness, the passion, the focus on cadence and stage presence as critical aspects of any verse worth reciting. This was a multiracial, multilingual chorus of voices, one founded on friendship, accident, and mutual respect of craft. They chose to share that unique, distinctly cosmopolitan vision with the world, and the results were spectacular. Algarín's mission was to create a space where ordinary people could experience the best parts of American poetry. For him, this meant that everyone—no matter what sort of job they did or didn't work, no matter their race, nationality, or level of education—could have the space to imagine. Performers and listeners alike got the chance to let their minds run free, to hear some of the freshest, most courageous voices in the city expound upon the most important matters of the day.

Newspapers and magazines from the period document this atmosphere in stunning detail, and often with an air of real admiration. Take, for example, this description from a 1978 essay by the Nuyorican poet Tato Laviera, "The Nuyorican Poets Cafe: A Workshop in Voices":

It is interesting to note that no where [*sic*] in the city of New York can a Poet find such an [intense] interaction between listener and Poet than at the Cafe. More incredible is the fact that poetry is sustained—supported for

such long periods of time. Unbelievable is the conclu-
sion that 75% of the Cafe's audience are young Lati-
nos straight out of Loisaida's stoops and abandoned
buildings. Why then this phenomena? Why then is this
old DECLAMACION tradition emerging in such an
unlikely place? The answer lies in the sound of written
words, the fact that the ear is the ghetto's most devel-
oped organ.

For Laviera, the essence of the spectacular performances that
take flight within the Cafe is a much older tradition of oral
performance within Puerto Rican culture, one that reappears
with renewed vigor in a neighborhood otherwise marked by
deprivation and neglect. This focus on the power of orality,
he claims, is not merely institutional but a kind of commu-
nal, cultural inheritance, a more widely shared way of being.
The emphasis is always on the ear: on a favorite song blaring
from the radio, a joke shared between friends, or a poem
read aloud in a crowded room.* This recognition resonates
with the people of Loisaida; they come out from all corners
of the neighborhood in the earliest days of the Cafe to hear
the intricacies of the world they know recited back to them,
beautified, and made new. Laviera opens the essay with a
scene that paints a picture of how this dynamic appeared
in real time: "It is Friday night, October 13, 1978, the Cafe

---

* In Pedro Pietri's words: "Free verse is the natural speech of the disenfranchised.
When people are down and out they become more musical with their words
because the sound of their voice keeps them going. All they have left is their
words."

is hot and humid. A new sound system and the mikes do not work. The room's west wall monopolized by the multi-talented Raúl Santiago Sebazco. His sketches in pencil are neatly framed next to his gigantic stoop-front painting . . . which serves as a background for the stage and all its readers." The Nuyorican, from its earliest days, was a site where visual art and spoken word collided to create an enthralling, audiovisual experience; a place for artists, across genres, to have their work seen and celebrated. But it was also a place for amateurs to learn and grow. Even when the speakers and microphones weren't working, or the air conditioning was out on the hottest day of the summer. Just as it was in the neighborhood, any active participant in the scene in those early days had to rely on a certain measure of inventiveness and a willingness to improvise. Even when everything around you seemed to be falling apart, you learned to make do, and how to do so in community.

The Nuyorican eventually became renowned for both its electric atmosphere and the expansive range of its featured poets. As news of the Cafe spread, it attracted talented writers from far outside the founders' circle. While Algarín and CienFuegos and Esteves and Pietri were there often, poets such as Allen Ginsberg and William S. Burroughs also read to crowds that packed the venue, anxious to experience the cutting-edge work of New York City's literary underground. These readings were live and direct and increasingly well attended, drawing crowds from across the city to see work tailored to no single set of aesthetic or political preferences but wild, thunderous, quiet, quixotic, explicitly political and profoundly personal, all sometimes within the scope of the same set. In that small room in Loisaida, you could see the full spectrum of joy and pain in human life reflected back to you. And a more beautiful world being built, line by line, each night.

Interlude: The Schoolroom

As far as I knew as a four-year-old boy, there was only one national anthem, and it opened with a call to collective action: "Lift every voice and sing." We sang the hymn—written at the turn of the century by James Weldon Johnson, with music composed by J. Rosamond Johnson—each morning from memory, me and the hundreds of other children from across the entire span of the African diaspora gathered in an auditorium that reflected the beauty of our blackness back to us. Earth-toned everything. Mahogany and maroon, ochre and sandalwood. Even my teacher's name, Ms. Cherry, seemed like a gesture toward both this shared proximity to the earth and a larger impetus toward sweetness, warmth, care. For although she was stern—and according to my big sister, my sworn enemy any time I ended up on an unjust time-out—Ms. Cherry, and all of the faculty I knew at the Modern School and walked alongside back then, treated us with respect and abiding tenderness. Our institutional pedagogy reflected this: every history and literature class explicitly celebrated the contributions of African American inventors, architects, educators, and activists. Everything we saw offered a vision of past, present, and future that not only included us but in fact asserted that we were pivotal actors in, an indelible part of, the narrative of human history.

The altogether uncommon nature of this arrangement was not yet evident to me, of course. At this point in my life, all I knew were environments akin to the one I entered every morning at West 152nd Street—a building purchased by educator Mildred Johnson Edwards in 1934, who started the Modern School, originally called the Ethical Culture School of Harlem, because she, the graduate of a teacher-training program at the Ethical Culture Society in Manhattan, "could not get a teaching position at any private school in the city."[11] This space, one of Harlem's earliest black private schools, was my first lesson in what school was, and what it could mean. I was raised in a black American home and lived in a neighborhood where almost everyone identified as Puerto Rican, Dominican, Cuban, Jamaican, or black American, and I attended a church with an Afroed Jesus adorning the walls of our Sunday-school classrooms. To my mind, if the Messiah was a black man, then what did I have to feel insecure or ashamed about? What social order worth its salt would dare to exclude me and my kin, my play cousins and closest friends? I had a place in the universe, secured by a constellation of brilliant, beautiful men and women strategically placed across space and time. I was a shimmering, albeit small, star in the grand design. I showed up in space and was recognized, reckoned with, and adored.

This was all, of course, before my family and I left town in 1992—six years before the Modern School was closed down and the building sold, due to financial struggles.[12] But back in 1992, it was still the first learning community I had ever known, and it would ultimately come to have a profound impact on the way I thought about the purpose, and promise, of an American education for years to come. Although I would never attend another institution that was quite like the Modern School in terms of its pedagogy or demographics, what remained with me for the rest of my days was the fact of what I felt in that building: an irreducible sense of belonging, and surety. And what's more, that we started each day with poems. The African American studies scholar and cultural historian Imani Perry has written about the history of "Lift Every Voice," originally written to honor the birthday of Abraham Lincoln:

> What James created with his lyrics stood in the tradition of a different February-born leader, the abolitionist author Frederick Douglass. Douglass, like most enslaved children, hadn't had his birth date recorded. However, he'd chosen February 14 as the day on which he would celebrate his birth. Not incidentally this was two days after Lincoln's. Frederick Douglass's narratives told the story of his journey from slavery to freedom with drama, passion, breathtaking emotion, and stunning brilliance. James's poem did something quite similar: he told the story of black life in terms that were epic, wrenching, and thunderous.[13]

The anthem for Lincoln's birthday, Perry concludes, "proved to be, both then and soon thereafter, much bigger than an ode to any one leader or icon. It was a lament and encomium to the story and struggle of black people. The Johnsons at once wrote black history and wrote black people into the traditions of formal Western music with their noble song."[14] Though I didn't know it yet, my Modern School peers and I were participating in a much longer tradition of black schoolchildren forging their connection to the national past through poetry, performance, and song. The anthem was an intimate part of this invisible ceremony. Without anyone saying so in explicit terms, we were asked to join an ever-expanding collective of elders and ancestors alike, a chorus of the living and the dead, who counted themselves as willing and able to assert black humanity in a landscape that denigrated them, and all that they held dear, from the very start. That poetry was the vehicle for this particular form of cultural education was no accident. Outside of the anthem itself, we were regularly encouraged to recite the poems of Gwendolyn Brooks, Paul Laurence Dunbar, Claude McKay, Maya Angelou, and a multitude of others. This combination of memorization and public performance was an act of both community building and active commemoration. By stepping into the voices of these poets, we were able to make the historical record come alive. We knew that these poems had power, and were meant to reflect our own power, our own possibility, back to us.

Each of our assigned poems had a sense of immediacy, and urgency, to them. Every line, even from the nineteenth-century poets such as Dunbar, felt to us like it could have been written by one of our parents or cousins. I still remember reciting: "Why should the world be over-wise, / In counting all our tears and sighs? / Nay, let them only see us, while / We wear the mask."[15] In that generative, transgenerational blur, that unfettered entanglement of historical actors and their language sent to us across the great expanse that we might live full, abundant lives, I learned a lesson I would never forget about the transformative power of poetic practice. We didn't recite poems to perform a certain level of esoteric, rarified knowledge. We read poems aloud to honor our heroes—and, if for only a fleeting moment, to *become* them. To take up their mantle and walk.

My beloved school, with its roots in the 1930s, was a distant cousin, in a sense, to the Black Arts Repertory Theatre/School (BARTS), an institution whose work and vision hovers in the background of whole modern spoken-word movement and was, chronologically, its immediate precursor.

Founded in Harlem in 1965 by Amiri Baraka, the institution dared to assert the possibility of an altogether divergent world, one where the cultural and artistic practices of black people all over the planet would be celebrated. It came into being as the embodiment of some of the black aesthetic tradition's most radical dreams: a school and events space dedicated to the cultivation of young black artists. At the core of their philosophy was the notion that not only black politics but black artistic practices were either actively ignored or else under attack in the United States. The institution was a response to this historical truth. And although BARTS existed for less than a year, it had an outsized impact on the arts landscape of its day. The space attracted artists such as the avant-garde saxophonist Albert Ayler, jazz composer and band leader Sun Ra, and poet Sonia Sanchez as teachers, and ultimately left an impact in the collective imaginations of both the young people of Harlem whom it immediately served and the countless other programs throughout the country that count it as an inspiration.

Baraka founded BARTS in the wake of Malcolm X's assassination. After Malcolm's death, Baraka changed his name from LeRoi Jones and set out to define the Black Arts Movement, which he rooted in the idea that black people across the world needed to establish their own aesthetics, a new vision of themselves freed from the constraints of the white imagination. Toward this end, Baraka not only founded BARTS, but partnered with Larry Neal and several other black writers to publish *Black Fire: An Anthology of Afro-American Writing*, which included the writings of thinkers like John Henrik Clarke, Harold Cruse, Kwame Ture, and others, as well as a foreword that outlined the basic tenets of the movement. BARTS was an extension of this larger philosophical commitment to black aesthetics, and used the performance of poetry as both an element of its pedagogy and one of its founding pillars. Its creation was indebted, in some sense, to other African American literary and political institutions tasked with a similar mandate: the creation of black art intimately bound up with our dreams of collective liberation.

One such collective from this historical period was the Umbra Workshop. Umbra was comprised entirely of black writers and based its operations on the Lower East Side. Its alumni included poets, scholars, and activists such as Ishmael Reed, Lorenzo Thomas, James Thompson, Askia M. Touré, Archie Shepp, Brenda Walcott, David Henderson, Steve Cannon, Tom Dent, Al Haynes, Calvin C. Hernton, Joe Johnson, Norman Pritchard, and Lennox Raphael. This group produced its own literary journal, *Umbra Magazine*, and would eventually split off into other, divergent factions, largely on the basis of ideological difference (the practice of writing as primary object and aim versus the literary arts as merely one arm of a larger revolutionary cause). Touré and Haynes in particular would go on to found one of these collectives, the Uptown Writers Movement. A number of the poets involved would eventually also join Baraka as faculty at BARTS, and contribute to that aspect of the school's character as an institution. Baraka's revolutionary vision was one in which the black underclass would find both the necessary psychic instruments to sustain themselves against anti-black ideology and the everyday skills needed to feed themselves. It was, explicitly, not art for art's sake. BARTS brought into the streets of Harlem the visible presence of the radical approach to art making that Baraka called for in his 1965 manifesto "The Revolutionary Theatre." Its broader purpose was essentially self-identical with that of the Black Arts Movement as such: to encourage a socially relevant form of black drama that would further build up the global struggle for a more equitable social order. The theater and school passionately advocated for black art in all its myriad forms, with dance recitals, poetry readings, visual-art shows, and new dramas created by the instructors.

The troupe brought the community into the theater through various means, including the well-known "Jazzmobile." Instructors from the school would drive the Jazzmobile up and down 130th Street, often enlisting black youth from the neighborhood to serve as library assistants, teaching assistants, stagehands, and maintenance men. These young people would eventually teach these crafts to children even younger than they were, creating, in their own way, a tradition within a tradition, a legacy of apprenticeship and childhood collaboration that would remain in the wake of any individual building or community institution. BARTS also brought the theater to the community by putting up improvised stages in playgrounds, parks, in empty parking lots and on street corners. Anywhere the people were gathered, they showed up and showed out.

For the faculty of BARTS, meaningful poetry, like outdoor theater, like meaningful education of any sort, was always tied up with contemporary politics, collective wellness, and the pursuit of justice. The BARTS faculty believed that the study of poetry and poetics did not have to be limited to a dominant cultural canon. One could produce, memorize, improvise, and perform poems, instead, in the style of the tradition that the Black Arts Movement poets were building together. To be clear, this sort of work was not explicitly referred to as "spoken word" at the time. But the style, the ethos, of these poetic performances served as clear precursors to the sound that would eventually operate under that banner. In both form and content, these performances served as a useful model—in New York and elsewhere—for the spoken word movement that would arrive in its wake.

A Party, Two Photographs, and a Parade

The second page of the May 4, 1965, edition of *Challenge*, the then-weekly newspaper produced by the Progressive Labor Party, tells the story of this photograph in miniature. The title of the article is "Black Arts School Set," and it details—in

cramped space, to be sure, but with vigor and a muted though unflinching optimism—the opening of the Black Arts Repertory Theatre/School on April 30, at 109 West 130th Street. The article describes an entire week of community events: a reading on the that day featuring Amiri Baraka, Ishmael Reed, Larry Neal, and others; a jazz concert; a panel, "The Black Artist and Revolution," featuring Cecil Taylor, Selma Sparks, and Harold Cruse, among others; an Off Broadway production of Baraka's play *The Toilet;* and, of course, the parade featured in the image above—a parade led, the article claims, by none other than the Albert Ayler Quartet, Baraka, and Sun Ra's legendary experimental jazz collective, the Arkestra. The final line of the article reads as follows: "Everyone was invited to join the opening weekend activities." This spirit of welcoming and collective endeavor characterized the early life of BARTS, and is captured, or set loose, in the grainy exuberance of this image of their inaugural public event, this festival to let folks know that a new way of reading the word and the world had arrived.

At its core, after all, Black art, at least as Baraka and his colleagues defined it, demands that we remember. The vision of Black Arts embodied in this moment of marching is a call back to a much longer tradition: one of black marshals and majors and bearers of banners of nations that live only in the freedom dreams of the marginalized. The flags of nations that have never existed and are yet to come. A captive nation *within* a nation.[16] Or "a nation on no map," if you prefer Gwendolyn Brooks's approach.[17] Or the America Langston Hughes calls into being in the fourteenth stanza of his classic poem "Let America Be America Again": "The land that has never been yet— / And yet must be."[18]

It is difficult to discern the identity of the man holding the flagpole in this photograph. The other, of course, is Amiri Baraka, wearing sunglasses and a jacket made of military canvas. The flag reads "The Black Arts Repertory Theatre/ School." A small procession follows the flag and the men who hold its body as it is carried toward West 130th Street. Here are Baraka's own words on that day and its larger significance:

> We rented a brownstone on W. 130th St. near Lenox, tore down the 1st floor walls and began our work. The announcement of our arrival in Harlem was a parade, with the small group of young Black artists, led by the great genius Sun Ra and his then Myth Science Arkestra. We still have photos of that. What the people of Harlem thought of that we would find out in various

ways as we travailed. But that was the opening. The weird, the interplanetary, the heliocentric world of Sun Ra, our syncopated point and I carried a brand new flag, designed by painter William White, the tragic/comic (like the earth, the south the smile of joy, the north the frown of sadness, dig it) dialectical mask of drama, fashioned into an African shield in black and gold. We walked all the way determined to make a revolution.[19]

In *The Challenge,* the attendant photo's annotation reads, "As a school it would set up and continue to provide instruction, both practical and theoretical, in all new aspects of the dramatic arts." Indeed, in addition to core classes in acting and poetry, the school also offered courses with titles such as Business Machines, Clerical Job Training, Cultural Philosophy, Psychology of Migration, and Social History of the West as well as classes in dance, cinema, music, and political science. Spanning an entire range of methods and disciplinary formations, the Black Arts Repertory Theatre/School registrar makes clear, in one sense, that Baraka's vision of what comprised a sound "anti-colonial" education—to borrow and reframe a phrase from Derek Walcott[20]—was quite unorthodox. The BARTS curriculum also included courses in remedial reading and mathematics, entries that, to my mind, clarify more completely the stakes and aims of the school itself. The goal was not solely to train a cadre of revolutionary artists, but to prepare a generation of young people to enter the world with any and every instrument they might need to flourish in an anti-black world. The aim was a robust liberal-arts education with an emphasis on the unheralded peoples of the planet Earth, and the cultivation of what Baraka then termed "socially responsible" citizens not only of "the ghetto" but of black communities everywhere.

Funding from the social activism organization Harlem Youth Opportunities Unlimited (HARYOU) and the Office of Economic Opportunity provided much of BARTS's support early on. Eventually, having so much of their financial support tied to these individual sources would help contribute to the school's tragic demise. BARTS was founded with the support of a $40,000 antipoverty grant, and eventually, following a concerted disinformation campaign, controversy erupted over such a flagrantly "anti-American"—at least in the minds of the school's detractors—use of public funds. In his autobiography, Baraka remembers the problem beginning when he denied Sargent Shriver, a founder of the Peace Corps and head of the Office of Economic Opportunity, entry into the BARTS building while school was in session. On November 30, 1965, the Associated Press sent out a release accusing the group of antiwhite racism, claiming that its productions supported secession and portrayed the general white American populace in a negative light. Several other published articles claimed that BARTS employed members of "black terrorist groups." The public outcry eventually culminated in an armed police raid on the brownstone building that reportedly uncovered firearms, drugs, bomb materials, and an underground gun range. Several representatives from HARYOU and other antipoverty programs defended the school's activities, arguing that young people in danger of criminal involvement were in actuality the very individuals the programs were intended to help. Despite these efforts, public funding all but disappeared. This absence of capital, coupled with internal disputes among the faculty and the premature exodus of Baraka, saw the collapse of the Black Arts Repertory Theatre/School by 1966.

Or at least this is the most familiar rendition of the story. But what if there were another rendition of the BARTS creation myth available to us, calling out from the gaps in the historical record? What version of this tale lives on in the darkness? In spaces unattended to, unthought, or altogether obscured from view? It is my sense that the most compelling, complete version of this tragedy has yet to be told, and can only be approached by reassembling the fragments and shards left in the wake of the school's untimely implosion. BARTS was a shining example, however short-lived, of the promise of arts-centered education for underserved communities.

We can now think of BARTS not just as a singular, isolated event—lightning in a brownstone, as it were—but as a nodal point in a much broader network of fugitive projects operating under the aegis of the black school as an alternative site of social life, one that stands as a countervailing force to the dominant vision of the American school as, in the first instance, an institutional mechanism through which the most violent whims of the settler imagination are instantiated and ingrained. It gives us the black arts school as a *figure*, of which BARTS was a fleeting, though nonetheless influential, concrete exemplar. The black school *as such* we can then see as the institutional arm of a much larger historical impetus anchored in the pursuit of black freedom and human dignity. I'm reminded of the classic line from Carter G. Woodson: "There would be no lynching if it did not start in the schoolroom."[21] This line of argumentation, a core element of Woodson's canonical 1933 text, *The Mis-Education of the Negro*, clearly served as a kind of meta-influence, even when it was not invoked explicitly, a guiding force of the central curriculum of BARTS, which was exceptionally expansive in its offerings. BARTS comes to us in the present, then, not as an institutional failure but instead as an unbound, unbroken meditation on how we might plan outside of the easy binary of success and failure we might recognize within our present order. BARTS represented a break in linear time: a briefest flash of who we can be, what we can accomplish, if we are brave.

It was not incidental that its founder was Baraka, twentieth- and twenty-first-century prophet of black fire, black self-determination, black life in a world dead set against its flourishing. In 1968, he recorded *Black & Beautiful, Soul & Madness* (1968), a record that merges jazz, scat rhythms, and oral poetry to stunning effect. *Black & Beautiful* served as Baraka's first foray into recorded work that would fuse live music and live recitation, and in this way helped lay the foundation for any number of spoken word artists that would come after him. In one sense, we might think of his poetics as the first steps toward a new grammar, a new set of aims, for spoken word performance. In an interview published in the fall 1980 issue of *The Greenfield Review*, he would say that his work was generally "intended to be read aloud, and since the mid-sixties that has been what has spurred it on, shaped it. . . . The page doesn't interest me that much—not as much as the actual spoken word." Public performance was at the center of it all.[22] Spoken word could become, not unlike it was in Langston Hughes's vision, a more democratic mode of engaging everyday folks in the work of making and sharing literature. Poetry would be the vehicle for liberatory politics, that which lent power, texture, to the freedom dreams of Baraka and his entire cohort.

I didn't always see Baraka's dream the way I do now. I met him for the first and last time in a crowded lecture hall in Cambridge, Massachusetts. We had both been invited to speak at Harvard University's 2009 Black Arts Festival on a panel concerned with the role of black aesthetics in our shared cultural moment. I was only somewhat familiar with the full breadth of his work at the time, and knew him primarily as an elder poet in a tradition I was still growing to understand through my English classes at Penn, as well my own practice as a poet and performance artist. I had very little real sense of the historical influence of the man seated next to me, and thus proceeded into our discussion and Q&A as only, perhaps, a brash twenty-year-old could: full of passion and certainty, laser-focused on the various lines of argumentation Baraka and my graduate-student colleague on the panel put forth, but with almost no context for what it truly meant to share that stage with him. And what's more—this more critically, perhaps—little sense of what the larger claims, historical and personal, he was making about the relationship between black art and political economy, political consciousness, and the substance of our collective aspirations truly meant for all of us gathered there.

As the hours sped past, it became clear that for the black-sweater-clad, unflinchingly eloquent elder statesman seated next to me, there was a necessary bridge between the art that black artists produced and the politics they espoused. If our art was not legibly tied to a particular kind of global, diasporic political project, then it was not *black art* at all, irrespective of the specific racial or ethnic identities of the people involved. This, to me, was an earth-shattering intervention. *That can't be right.* Just about everything I heard Baraka say that afternoon flew directly in the face of the way I had been trained to think at that point. Characteristically (though I did not know to read it this way at the time), Baraka remained firm in his convictions, and his claim, over and against the audible disagreement of both me and the majority of the crowd in attendance, that *it's not black art if it's not for the People.*

From his vantage, the truth of the matter was clear and undeniable. I left the room unconvinced. It was only through years of subsequent study—both in graduate school and in informal reading groups that would change the trajectory of my life as a scholar and writer—that I would come to understand the true power of Baraka's argument, as well as its centrality to his life and legacy. Whatever the social and political role of black art was, it did in fact exist in excess of any identity position I could name or lay claim to. There was a kind of atmospheric pull, a honed, critical energy moving against traditional notions of property and propriety alike that this thing called black aesthetics was calling us toward instead. A different way of thinking of the ostensible boundary between a single person and the People. Between aesthetic expression and political possibility. Between movement work and the work of art.

"Why do we do politics?" Baraka once asked, in an interview recorded toward the end of his life and focused centrally on his newfound craft as a painter. "To protect truth and beauty." As it was in the end, so it was in the beginning. And so he built. And so they came from all across the city to see what he and his friends had made. In their hands, the craft of teaching poetry and live performance was not merely about the expression of a self-contained, self-possessed subject, but the rallying cry for every black human being willing to embrace the idea that they are altogether inextricable from a larger constellation of witnesses, bound together by the beauty and terror of the world within worlds we share. There were any number of Black Arts poets during this period crafting work that blurred the boundaries between preaching and poetry, chant and speech, in ways that would inform spoken word aesthetics for years to come. Chief among them was one Nikki Giovanni.

Giovanni's first album, *Truth Is On Its Way*, was meant to serve as a reparative measure of sorts. And not merely the kind that might attend to the divide between the literary establishment and the reading public—or else between rival factions of contemporary writers—but a record for those who had been left behind, or else ignored, by all of these groups. In Giovanni's own words: "I wanted something my grandmother could listen to and I knew if gospel music was included, she would listen. I have really been gratified with the response of older people, who usually feel that black poets hate them and everything they have stood for. The record demonstrates that this isn't so."

She was clearly on to something. The first live reading of her poems, a free concert at Canaan Baptist Church in Harlem, packed out. Fifteen hundred people gathered in the space to hear the new work. Giovanni's strategic melding of popular forms worked to great effect outside the realm of live performance as well; the album would go on to sell 100,000 copies in the first six months following her reading.

For decades, Giovanni, who once wrote that a poet should "write the way [they] breathe" would continue to produce work that further blurred the distance between written poetry, live performance, and an entire range of musical stylings including blues, jazz, and gospel. The public performance of this poetry could also now be used as a means of attending to generational wounds. The craft was no longer simply or primarily a weapon against enemies but a way of inviting our friends, old and new, to unify.

How might we situate Giovanni's performance, as well as the content and reception history of her best-selling album, within a larger history of African American preaching, spoken word performance, and everyday black political practice? What can we learn from her willingness to blend a genre like gospel music with the ostensibly secular vision and purpose of something like performance poetry? Rather than assigning assumptions of retrograde or conservative thinking to social sites like the black church, Giovanni demands that we take into consideration the totality of the communities we come from, adore, and hope to transform.

Public responses to Giovanni's decision to leap into the

world of collaborative albums were mixed (outright criticism from Baraka, and a review in *Black World* of her second album, *Like a Ripple on the Pond*, which stated that "the feeling of fire and commitment [from her earlier work] is gone"). But Giovanni held firm to her conviction that such performances were absolutely central to her larger, intellectual project:

> It would be ridiculous, the only word I can think of, that I would live in an electronic age and not choose to electronically transmit my voice. . . . I think that our obligation is to use whatever technology is available, because whether or not art is able to be translated tells us something about whether or not it's, in fact, living, whether or not it's part of us.[23]

Both on wax and in the moment of performance, *Truth Is On Its Way* gives us an updated, uncompromising vision of the black poet as preacher, spoken word as a cord connecting sermon and lyric. It reminds us that the future life of black poetics depends on our willingness to turn to the past, to the chorus calling to us from the archive, demanding not only that we remember, but that we bear witness.

What is the relationship between blackness and place? Blackness and drama? Black drama and the making of a world at the end of the world, one that is insuperable and invisible, some miniature cosmos encased in the armor of the everyday, kept secret from the eyes of the dominant class, kept precious in the fellowship halls, black-box theaters, and middle-school classrooms where children and their teachers would memorize lines together and endeavor to become what they were told they were not, had never been, could never be?

Can we think of Harlem, then, as a fundamentally dramatic place, as a space of literature and music and theater and poetry brought to life—animated by breath, and a perfectly timed pause, and brown fingertips etching scenes of human endeavor onto the smooth black air—but also in the sense that Zora Neale Hurston imagined in her timeless essay "Characteristics of Negro Expression"? There, she writes: "The Negro's universal mimicry is not so much a thing in itself as an evidence of something that permeates his entire self. And that thing is drama. His very words are action words. His interpretation of the English language is in terms of pictures. One act described in terms of another."[24] The Black Arts Repertory Theatre/School represented the institutionalization of a long-standing impulse: the daily drama of black life, its implicit performative powers, given architectural form.

And though BARTS existed for less than a calendar year, it stands as a historical monument to what I would like to imagine here as a kind of *black temporality:* life measured not in minutes but in moments. Black social life itself an everyday, ongoing set of practices and protocols rooted in the fact that we all ultimately lose what we love, and thus must embrace loss, embrace love, not as antipodal, irreconcilable forces, but as irreducibly bound up with each other, entangled like the individual obsidian coils of a baby cousin's braid, or the internal wiring of a microphone on a makeshift stage from which that child will recite an ode to their neighborhood corner—Lenox or Nostrand or King's Boulevard—at the very top of their dark and holy voice, as if it were the most urgent, pressing news any listening audience could imagine, or else a trumpet to signal the end of the world and the dawning of another.

The Two Miguels

Out of all the characters, all the complex, lifelong relationships in the spaces Algarín helped create in the early days of the Nuyorican Poets Cafe, there was a specific bond that best exemplifies the wild trajectory of spoken word poetry in the period between the opening of the living room in 1973 and the official reopening of the brick-and-mortar Nuyorican Poets Cafe in '89: his relationship with the rebel artist Miguel Piñero, who turned up at Algarín's place before the move to the Sunshine Tavern, after years spent in and out of prison. Fresh off a bid at Sing Sing, Piñero found in Algarín's living room a space where he would sharpen his work habits, build up his name, and reenter the world as a poet and playwright born anew from the ash. The tale of these two men is, in one sense, the tale of this particular window of the twentieth-century spoken-word movement in miniature: an ode to the social and political possibilities that emerge when undeniable stories, from unexpected places, are given their proper due.

On one side, there was the buttoned-up, formally educated Professor Miguel: the institutionally minded, doubly conscious trailblazer, marking the parameters of a new canon. The embodiment of his mother's dreams, and by extension, the dreams of millions of other, unnamed mothers, many of whom could or would not dare to envision their sons taking the songs of their dilapidated, perpetually neglected *barrios* to the broader world. On the other side was Miguel the Rebel: the formerly incarcerated enfant terrible. The misinterpreted, miseducated genius.

Miguel Piñero was born in 1946, in the small town of Gurabo, Puerto Rico. He came to the United States when he was four years old, with his parents, Adelina Piñero and Miguel Angel Gómez, and his sister. His mother was an amateur fiction writer, and even as they struggled, a certain commitment to literary pursuit was always in the air. Four years after the family had permanently relocated to the Lower East Side from Puerto Rico, Piñero's father would abandon the family unexpectedly. Miguel Sr. never returned. His namesake was only eight years old at the time. In the wake of his father's departure, young Piñero struggled mightily. Unable to financially support the family on her own, Adelina Piñero was forced to move with her children into the basement of a friend's home, where they spent a fair portion of his childhood. At the outset of his teenage years, Miguel spent much of his time shoplifting with other kids from the neighborhood. At thirteen, he joined a local gang known as the Dragons; Piñero would later admit to committing over one hundred robberies during this especially tempestuous stage of his life—sometimes for sport, but most of the time to procure food for his family to eat that night. In seventh grade, he decided to drop out of school altogether. After that, he was in and out of juvenile detention centers for the next five years, serving time at the Otisville State Training School for Boys and the Juvenile Detention Center in the Bronx. At the age of eighteen, Piñero was sentenced to serve time for armed robbery, and summarily sent to Rikers Island. He was on his third prison sentence by the age of twenty-four. He had just been released from his second stint inside when he found out about Algarín's living room.

There is a real peculiarity and power to Piñero's story. In so many ways, his arc as a writer truly exemplified the transformative potential of spoken word. He spent the entirety of his childhood toeing the tightrope between life and death, survival and starvation, and yet somehow eventually became a bona fide icon of the spoken word movement. He is noteworthy in this regard, but he is not alone. The legacy of the Nuyorican features many other figures who likewise rose from difficult circumstances to pursue a life of creative expression and, ultimately, social and cultural transformation. Put another way, although Piñero is certainly a standout among the Nuyorican's founders, he represents much of what is so special about the group as a whole. Each and every one of these poets was in one way or another breaking new ground in the American literary scene. As a collective, they helped democratize the nation's vision of poetry and poetics by creating a space where anyone—former inmates, activists, fledgling professors—could have the chance to write in community and to be heard.

In between the brutal, formative years that he spent on the inside, this period of Miguel Piñero's life was marked by his movement between any number of wildly divergent institutions in the outside world: Camp Kilmer, Phoenix House, and Manhattan State Hospital, where he would eventually earn his GED after his second stint on Rikers Island. Looking in on his life from the outside now, it appears agonizingly clear that Piñero had given himself over in this moment to the process of becoming something, someone, fundamentally different than he had ever been, and this by any means available to him. Even as a boy of nineteen, finally out of the system if only for a moment, Piñero was committed to transformation, reform, and radical political activity. He joined the revolutionary organization known as the Young Lords, perhaps in an attempt to help keep other young people from the neighborhood from going down a similarly destructive path. Whether it was rehab, radicalism, the Job Corps, or the US Army, he seemed willing to try his hand at whatever method, whatever way of life, might liberate him, or at least set him on a trajectory toward a totally different path.

During his final years in prison, beginning in Sing Sing in 1971, something clicked. While there, he made the decision to join a prison theater workshop and acting troupe popularly known as the Family. The group was founded by two nonincarcerated professional actors named Clay Stevenson and Marvin Felix Camillo; the latter would play a central role in Piñero's growth while in the workshop as well as in his trajectory as a poet, playwright, and provocateur during his life on the outside. Indeed, it was while living and working in the midst of this performance collective that Piñero produced what would be the most exciting, widely acclaimed work of his brief but indelibly impactful career. His first published poem, a strange, irreducibly problematic work of free verse entitled "Black Woman with the Blond Wig On," was entered into a contest by Camillo and earned Piñero fifty dollars—the first money he had ever earned from putting pen to paper. For his entire life up to that point, he had never held a steady job, and now, from out of nowhere, this new vista opened up. This was not the true turning point of Piñero's career, however. That came with the publication of his magnum opus, the dramatic work *Short Eyes*.

In 1972—around the same time that Miguel Algarín was collaborating with Joseph Papp, and Esteves was on her way to discovering the scene at Algarín's place—the *New York Times* theater critic Mel Gussow visited Sing Sing. During that trip, he watched an entire series of plays both written and acted by Piñero. The work astonished him. For the next decade, Gussow would go on to review and offer critical praise of Piñero's work in print. This kind of reception, in the paper of record no less, transformed Piñero's life. Once released from prison, he joined back up with various members of the Family as part of a larger program being held at the Theatre of the Riverside Church in Harlem. This version of the theater troupe was composed primarily of formerly incarcerated men and recovering opioid users. Here, Piñero, still working primarily with Marvin Camillo, would rework *Short Eyes*, honing it through rehearsal, collective editing, and blocking that Camillo himself would later describe as both deeply rigorous and thoroughly improvisational. It was at this point that Piñero took an active leadership role in the life of the Family. He became the director of Third World projects for the Theatre of the Riverside and oversaw the inclusion of a wide range of productions created by black and brown playwrights attempting, not unlike him, to make a lasting impact on a genre in which historically they had been ignored or from which they had been outright barred.

Even in its earliest stages, many of those involved knew

that *Short Eyes* was going to be a hit. The Artistic Director of the Theatre of the Riverside Church, Arthur Bartow, eventually arranged to produce *Short Eyes* and bring it to a larger audience. After its 1974 premiere at Riverside, the play would move first to Joe Papp's Public Theater and eventually to the Vivian Beaumont Theater at Lincoln Center. Later that year, it won a New York Drama Critics Circle Award and an Obie Award for best Off Broadway play and earned a Tony nomination for Best Play. In 1977, a film version of the play—which included Piñero as one of the actors—hit the silver screen.

Alongside his widespread fame in the theater sector, the late seventies and early eighties were also a time when Piñero's labors were being recognized by the mainstream American academy. He was invited to speak at Princeton University, Rutgers University, and the Pratt Institute to large lecture halls of students and professors alike. Shortly after the debut of *Short Eyes*, he began to turn much of his attention toward mentoring Puerto Rican youth in the same area where he grew up, transforming the apartment he purchased with proceeds from the play into an informal space of outreach and community arts mentorship. One of these students was the American playwright Reinaldo Povod, whose critically acclaimed first play, *Cuba and His Teddy Bear* (1986), starring Robert De Niro, would win a George Oppenheimer/Newsday Award.

The tradition Piñero started by both writing and acting in *Short Eyes* would continue throughout his career. He acted in all of the plays he wrote, and even had the opportunity to appear in a fairly wide range of films throughout the 1980s. His filmography includes but is not limited to *Times Square* (1980), *Fort Apache, the Bronx* (1981), *Breathless* (1983), *Exposed* (1983), *Deal of the Century* (1983), *Alphabet City* (1984), and *Almost You* (1984). Sadly, in many of these films Piñero appeared only briefly—most often in roles that were, on their face, exaggerated distortions of the characters who populated the worlds of his poetry and plays. His television roles in *Kojak, Baretta,* and *Miami Vice* during this period seemed to fall into the same trap: more often than not, if you had the chance to catch him onscreen it was in the role (and sometimes even a recurring one, as was the case in *Miami Vice*) of the vice lord, the con man, the drug dealer. In addition to this reliable work as a character actor, he also worked on set as a "street dialogue" script specialist. What makes matters complicated, however, is that Piñero wrote any number of these roles *for and by himself.*

The 2001 film *Piñero* (where Piñero is played by Benjamin Bratt, of *Law & Order* fame) depicts a scene in which, in the late eighties, Piñero stole Miguel Algarín's television (Algarín is played masterfully by Giancarlo Esposito) from his apartment while he was out of town, and attempted to sell it for thirty-five dollars or so—in his own words, "to buy a new liver." After he lifts the television from Algarín's living room, we witness a series of shots where our disheveled protagonist attempts to sell the device in the middle of Avenue A, to no avail, hailing passersby with his own amalgam of improvised poetry and auctioneer speech. Eventually a couple, man and woman, stop to hear him out. The pair discuss the potential purchase back and forth before eventually deciding to buy the clearly used television set, if only because, one quips, "we need one for the bathroom anyway." When Piñero playfully responds to this remark with his trademark, profanity-infused humor, the couple, strangely enough, admonish him to "be cool" and "take that filthy language somewhere else."

In this scene, as in numerous others throughout the film, we see firsthand the brutal duality of Piñero's life at this juncture. He survived childhood poverty and a multiple-year stint in Sing Sing, only to achieve literary fame and lose it all within the span of a decade. The same raw language that brought him critical acclaim, and fleeting economic independence, in this scene marks him as a crass outsider who never quite knows how to read the room. The pain, the sense of humor, and the penchant for high drama that draw people to Piñero are also what ultimately alienate him from them. He is bearable, it appears, only in specific contexts and controlled doses. "Anyone could be a poet the way you live," Algarín exclaims in a moment of rage aimed toward the young Piñero, this argument springing to life once he comes home and discovers what his friend has done: "I could write like you if I didn't have to worry about working, and sleeping, and paying the rent." Here, a bright ray of envy pierces through. And something more than envy as well. The film's director, Leon Ichaso, tells stories about reported encounters with Piñero on the set of *Miami Vice* that echo much of the complicated, dynamic, undeniably compelling man he depicts in the film:

> Years later, working on *Miami Vice,* I heard many sto-
> ries about when he was on the show, the special kind
> of security measures that the production would take

to ensure he would not disappear or sneak into the wardrobe department, and then hold a shoe sale the next day. But Michael Mann, the director who created *Miami Vice,* respected Piñero a lot, as a writer and as a person. He had worked with him on his first film, way before *Miami Vice.* . . . Our paths crossed again, and I met with him while casting a film. You never knew what was going to happen when he and his friends came into the room. But I got even more interested when I was having dinner with a group of people and the Miguel Piñero stories started flying.[25]

Ichaso continues, clarifying that at a certain point, all the stories he had heard about Piñero became an inspiration to study the actual work; to get a better sense of what manner of brilliance inspired this level of mythmaking:

I started reading Piñero; yeah he's a madman, but also a wonderful writer who was falling through the cracks. *Short Eyes* was no longer in print, his poetry was difficult to get, his plays were produced less and less and I realized that soon there wasn't going to be a trace of him. I thought, Jesus, what a shame—somebody that was so influential in the '70s, one of the people responsible for spoken word as we know it today, who used to do his poetry with music. Plus it was a fascinating life. He became as much a New Yorker as anybody else and yet his is also the story of uprooted men who started a life here without forgetting where they came from.[26]

Miguel Piñero's brilliance is inextricably tied, in his own mind and the minds of others, to what is read, when he is down on his luck, as bad behavior, but at any other time is interpreted as little more than a kind of permissible eccentricity—the true calling card of any performance artist worth his salt. What would the man be worth, after all, without his all-too-common anguish and irrefutably uncommon talent, or the painful, profitable tales that emerged from their peculiar union in his body? Who would he be without the agony he inflicts on himself, but also extends beyond the province of his individual life and into the worlds of those around him? The work itself leads us toward a potential set of answers. Consider, for instance, one of Piñero's best-known poems from a collection of the same name, "La Bodega Sold Dreams":

> dreamt i was a poet
> &
> writin' silver sailin' songs
> words
> strong & powerful crashin' thru
> walls of steel & concrete
> erected in minds weak
> &
> those asleep
> replacin' a hobby of paper candy
> wrappin', collectin'
> potent to pregnate sterile young
> thoughts

i dreamt i was this poeta
words glitterin' brite & bold
strikin' a new rush for gold
in las bodegas
where our poets' words & songs
are sung
but
sunlite stealin' thru venetian
blinds
eyes hatin', workin' of time
clock
sweatin'
&
swearin'
&
slavin'
for the final dime
runnin' a maze
a token ride

perspiration insultin' poets
pride
words stoppin' on red
goin' on green
poets' dreams
endin' in a factoria as one
in a million
unseen
buyin' bodega sold dreams . . .[27]

Piñero's title poem is rooted, as is so much of his work, in a poetics of demolition. In his dream of being a poet, the "silver sailin' songs" we might at first be tempted to read as vessels of transport—to a utopian elsewhere, perhaps, or at least to the briefest respite from the gruesome order of things implied by a more pessimistic reading of the poem's title, a world where capitalism haunts us *even as we sleep*—turn out to be battleships, land-borne instruments of war intended to break through, sail over, the constraints of a world dead set against the imaginations of everyday people. From this destruction, the speaker of Piñero's poem asserts, will come new life, new possibilities for the impoverished masses he describes at length throughout the poem's second and third stanzas. The people who have little time, the reader might imagine, for poetry. Those whose relationship to the beauty of the quotidian is ensnared by the long arm of the bosses, and their necessarily extractive theory of time. Instead of writing, the workers populating Piñero's poem are "sweatin' & swearin' & slavin'" (this moment of tripled alliteration calling to mind the "silver sailin' songs" of the first stanza). Their exploitation doesn't end at the factory door.

By the poem's end, Piñero decides to fan out, painting a much larger picture of a citizenry "unseen": the millions of black and brown people who show up at the neighborhood bodega on a daily basis not only to hear their songs—and thus implicitly the most intimate textures of their intricate, precarious lives repeated back to them—but to play at one day entering the realm of the seen and accounted for. This anticipates not only what the future of spoken word would look, and sound, like but who would tell the tale.

The life of a craftsman was, for Piñero, a protracted gambit. He had a one-way pass out of state prison and into a world where the very experiences that had once made him a criminal, an enemy of the carceral state, would now make him a darling of the mainstream theater world. All this without having to change the way he dressed, or spoke, or approached the Sisyphean work of building an oeuvre from the void. In this respect, the precedent embodied in Piñero's trajectory is significant for spoken word artists down through the kids I met at the Nuyo in the 2000s. Which, based on the writing that has survived Piñero—and not just the poems from his own pen, but the writings about him and the way he flew through the world of Loisada in his heyday, an archangel engulfed in flame—was an experience not unlike the somewhat unfathomable everyday shift that comes with winning the lottery. For Piñero, and for us as contemporary listeners to the long and ongoing story of spoken word in America, the symbol of the lotto ticket also cuts in other directions. It's an indicator of abjection, pointing us toward the difficult truth of just how limited the life chances are for this historically underserved, undertheorized population of New Yorkers. What does it mean to hinge one's immediate future on such improbable odds, and count that wager as a revered social practice? "La Bodega Sold Pipe Dreams" hovers as a phantom title, just in the background. La bodega sold hoop dreams . . . la bodega sold dreams of another America—one that never has been, and yet, we imagine, must nonetheless be on its way.

Part of what Piñero uncovers in this, one of his best-known poems, is the *cruel optimism*, to use Lauren Berlant's phrase, of the age-old game so many denizens of Loisada are coerced into playing, the countless first-generation community members like the family and friends he grew up watching die on these very same streets.[28] The dreams the bodega sells can break your spirit, if you aren't careful—if they are not interpreted with care and more than a bit of caution.

Though the success of *Short Eyes* helped inaugurate key changes in Piñero's life, becoming a famous playwright did little to interrupt his ongoing struggles with the law. In 1974, three years before the Hollywood debut of *Short Eyes*, he was arrested for cursing at a subway attendant during an underground confrontation between the two. The year of the debut, Piñero was arraigned on charges of grand larceny and drug possession at the Tombs prison—another one of the many New York City carceral institutions he came to know during his life—while the film's director, Robert M. Young, was filming various scenes elsewhere throughout the prison. Piñero would eventually appear in the film as a character named Go-Go, but miss its debut while he was incarcerated, after being arrested again for grand larceny. In 1983, he went in for heroin possession. The trouble Piñero illustrated so evocatively on the written page followed him all throughout his life. Even as he lay dying, the man found a way to translate his anguish into verse. His final work, the unfinished play *Every Form of Refuge Has Its Price,* takes place in the intensive-care unit of a New York City hospital. In 1988, at the age of forty-one, he died of cirrhosis. His funeral was a poetry reading of grand scale and ambition, with guests ranging from Amiri Baraka and Sonia Sanchez to none other than Algarín himself, reading an elegy for Piñero. His ashes were scattered where they truly belonged: all over the landscape of Loisaida.

The danger of dreams, dreams deferred and lost and found again, is a central theme of the works in which Miguel Algarín's and Miguel Piñero's lives overlap. The most resonant of these, perhaps, is the final poem in Algarín's striking 1997 collection, the aptly titled, especially given our present investigation, *Love Is Hard Work*. It's an elegy for Piñero, "On Seeing Miky's Body":

> (7th street and Avenue A)
> What the hell are you
> doing in there?
> Your lips sewn,
> Your eyelids shut
>   for
>   ever.
> What do you think you're doing
> Hidden in that casket?
> Come out, come on out
> and let's play,
> what's a guy to do
> without you, without CienFuegos,
> without his main mellow men?
> Who's a guy to play with?
> Make words with.
> Got to get you back!
> How come you let me go,
> Didn't I love you
> with the right "e"
> Not the one for empty,
> But the one for enough,

the one for eternally,
like I'm eternally yours,
you eternally mine,
but now, now you can't
come play with me
in Tompkins Square Park,
and I can't get mad at you?
Figure that one out!
Who am I going to be mad at?
Damn you take a lot of liberties
Leaving me in Loisaida
With all my planets atwirl,
silly like a spinning child,
swirling and straining,
and crying too,
like the day I was chasing you
in Tompkins Square Park
    to make you stop saying
      what you were saying about me,
      I don't remember now
      what you were saying about me,
I don't remember now
what it was you were saying,
but I skinned my knee
trying to catch up to you
and what would I have done
had I caught up to you
    except shake you and hug you
and jump into our usual jump-rope,

just you and me, and Lucky skipping,
twirling the rope faster and faster
till we could shout at him
you're out
at which point Lucky would say
"it beez that way sometimes
And even after I die,
It'll be that way always"[29]

The emotional through line of the poem is a series of persistent back-and-forths: between childhood and adulthood, the cradle and the grave, outright rage and the unleashed, unremitting melancholy which serves as its structural foundation. There is a palpable sense of loss here, yes, but also the repeated implication that it was not only Piñero's brilliance, his genre-defying works and casual facility with language, that bound these two men. Not quite. It was his antics, his silliness, his consistent, categorical refusal to adhere to the rules, unspoken and otherwise, of both the profession and polite society more broadly, which brought and ultimately held them together in their inextricable roles: the two are playground collaborators and devoted co-admirers, people who jump rope and "make words with" one another. Even at the time of writing this, almost a decade after his friend's death in 1988, Algarín is still in search of words to describe what Piñero represents to him, and the larger cultural movement he has dedicated his life to. He is the last man standing. No Lucky, no Miky, no mellow main men left to share the occasion of the work they invested in for years growing,

shape-shifting, making its mark as a truly global phenom-
enon. The poem opens on Seventh Street and Avenue A and
leaves us there to wait out eternity.

Algarín closes *Love Is Hard Work* with not one, but an
entire series of elegies. Along with "On Seeing Miky's Body,"
there are poems for Lucky CienFuegos, as well as the poets
Michael St. Clair and Michael Skolnick, among others who
were there in the early days on Sixth Street. *Love Is Hard Work*
can be read, in one sense, as a book of elegies, a sequence of
attempts at recalling the social circle the great man has lost
over the years, a litany of the dead that must end with Piñero,
though with Lucky's words, and on the Lower East Side, giv-
ing the stories of their too-short lives over to the texture of the
printed page. There, Algarín is also able to do what he always
has done best: the sharing of submerged public histories. In
resurrecting the writers and dancers of his beloved Loisaida—
the one he remembers and revivifies each time he speaks, that
which still thrives, somehow, just beneath the pavement and
the luxury condos and cafés adorning it, masquerading as a
wondrous and irresistible future—Algarín demands that we
engage fully with the worlds we lost, the worlds *we are yet
losing*. We must remember these women and men, the revo-
lutions they saw come and go, the sounds they perfected as
the city burned and was reborn anew all around them. The
literary critic and poet made a case for the importance of an
archival impulse in an age obsessed with forgetting—a case
manifest in the poetry, as well as in Algarín's social relations.
At its core, the Nuyorican Poets Cafe is a place he built for
his friends. Because he believed in their craft, and what it
could ultimately accomplish on the global stage, yes, but also

more fundamentally as a labor of love. A title is a door into the unfamiliar. Love is hard work indeed.

Loisaida was many places at once: a global community both imagined and concrete which lives through the writers that call these disparate locations home and imbue them with the spirit of the origin point. Loisaida is something you carry inside you. Etymologically, it is a Spanglish fusion of "Lower East Side" and "Loiza," a town on the northeastern coast of Puerto Rico that, in the words of Ed Morales, "is widely acknowledged as the heart of African culture on the island."[30] It is a mode of being in and toward the world, an orientation toward the relationship between practice and recitation, community gathering and political activity of all kinds. Algarín's status as a major figure in this movement is not marked primarily, if at all, by the quality or critical duration of his work on the page. Rather, what constitutes his position of renown within this wing of the tradition is the *spiritual* work, to use Ishmael Reed's framing, that he undertook over the course of almost fifty years. Over and against the forms of mainstream media that might, overtly or otherwise, work to erase much of what he and his cohort contributed to the present literary arts landscape, Algarín demands we remember, through ode and elegy and community vigils, to mourn the dead. We write poems, in the Nuyorican tradition, both to remember where we have been and to map out a vocabulary in direct conflict with the amnesiac influence of our present order. All with the aim of altering the way our society might approach the work of making poems, thinking about poetics, in the broadest possible sense. To view it as everyday activity. A daily sharpening of the imagination, undertaken by ordinary people all around the world, across the spectrum of divergent identities and political affiliations. Algarín and company were always building an arts movement, whether they knew it or not. They were always going to need, at a certain point, more room to do right by the vision. Which, of course, is why they eventually needed a building. It is also why they made sure, at every turn, to honor the inauguration of the movement in their relationships as comrades, collaborators, and friends.

After Miky Piñero was gone, Algarín would be there to carry forward the legacy and find ways to spread the good news of spoken word, to distill the energy of the movement they'd helped to create in ways that were legible to everyday people as well as the tastemakers of New York City publishing. One of the more salient, however belated, examples of this sort of savvy on his part was the 1994 publication of the poetry anthology *Aloud: Voices from the Nuyorican Poets Cafe*. In it, we are able to witness both the sheer width of the spectrum of the writers who now represent the long tradition of Nuyorican poetics (a transgenerational, transnational, multiethnic coalition of writers as aesthetically diverse as one could imagine), as well as a compelling narrativization of the movement's vision regarding its still-nascent relationship to an ever-expanding audience. A review of the anthology by poet and scholar Thomas Swiss offered the following critique: "Although the poems collected here do indeed suggest a kind of American Cafe poem, they nevertheless owe something not only to the current crop of American rappers but to the Beat poets who read nightly (sometimes accompanied by jazz) at City Lights Bookstore in San Francisco in the 1950s. What was important to the literary bohemia of that time is

apparently still important to the bohemia of the moment—
the notion that poetry should reach a large audience and be
'democratic.'" Swiss quotes Algarín as saying that poetry
should be meaningful, but not without also being "fun," and
that it should be "televised."[31]

For Algarín, across the years, there was no shame in the
mass popularization of poetry. Quite the opposite: one of the
triumphs of the Nuyorican movement was that, as the café
evenings became more popular in the early 1990s, its wave
rising as hip-hop music became the sound of a generation,
the work was reaching more people than ever before, and
beyond that, it was deemed, above all else, *enjoyable*. This
is a meaningful distinction between Algarín and any num-
ber of his peers, including those anthologized in *Aloud*. The
potential he saw in spoken word was not limited to a popu-
list cultural politics or even the creation of a more diverse,
international coalition of literary voices. These were worthy
aims, to be sure. But Algarín was also interested in the dance
between political poetry and the realm of *mass entertainment*.
Somehow, despite having devoted his entire life to creative
pursuits one might read as utterly antithetical to the realm
of popular culture (elite academe on the one hand and liter-
ary poetry on the other), through his experiences as a curator
of performance at the Nuyorican Poets Cafe, Algarín tapped
into a truth of the moment that would change everything
about the way this craft that he loved would be disseminated
in the years to come. He realized, long before many oth-
ers, that he and his sisters and brothers were uniquely posi-
tioned to make art with unlimited, yet perennially untapped,
crossover potential—and eventually, with mainstream, truly

global appeal. As Swiss alludes to in his review, by the early nineties the Nuyorican sound was clearly operating in both a sonic and a discursive space forged at the intersection of Beat poetry and hip-hop. Having emerged, chronologically, at the midpoint of these two cultural revolutions, Nuyorican poetry captured some of the most intriguing, transformational aspects of both worlds. Eventually, however, the Nuyorican perspective on spoken word would run up against an ongoing conflict with the worlds of both publishing and elite institutions. Swiss writes: "Perhaps the biggest challenge this anthology brings readers is trying to fill in what's missing from its pages—that is, the poets' performances. Since spoken word is composed to be spoken, this new oral poetry, when confined to the page, over-emphasizes the literary elements of the text and makes unavailable readings that account for the collaborative involvement of audience in shaping the poetic text."[32]

The sheer range of these sorts of performances was captured to dazzling effect in the Italian filmmaker Costanzo Allione's *Fried Shoes Cooked Diamonds* (1979), which was filmed during the summer of 1978 at the Naropa Institute in Boulder, Colorado. The film features an assortment of distinctive voices in twentieth-century American poetry, bringing together the energy of the Beats and the Nuyoricans: William S. Burroughs, Allen Ginsberg, Peter Orlovsky, Anne Waldman, Diane di Prima, Timothy Leary, Daniel Ellsberg, Amiri Baraka. And then right around the 23:30 mark in the film, the singing voice of Miguel Piñero echoing out from the screen seemingly ex nihilo; he's wearing a sleeveless cream tank top and a gold ring. The camera swiftly pivots to

the source of the voice we hear harmonizing behind Piñero, and it's Algarín in a teal dashiki, salt-and-pepper Afro and mustache. "Now there's oratory" we hear Ginsberg, the film's narrator, opine over the honeyed baritone harmony filling the room. Ginsberg describes Piñero as possessing an "American New York junkie been-in-jail energy street voice, loud street voice that can be heard, the rhythms are so definite and Puerto Rican," just before characterizing Algarín as a "professor of Shakespeare at Rutgers in New Jersey, proprietor of the Nuyorican Poets Cafe on East Sixth Street on the Lower East Side."[33] This juxtaposition is striking, in no small part because it follows a scene roughly ten minutes earlier where Ginsberg similarly talks over a spellbinding performance by

Amiri Baraka of his poem "Afro-American Lyric," making a joke—"I wonder if he's going to say anything horrible, declare revolution now"—as Baraka offers a critique of capitalism, racism, and sexism before moving into the reading. To be sure, there's a certain anxiety that seems to underpin Ginsberg's narration of Baraka's performance, as well as Piñero and Algarín's in particular, especially in his claim that there is a "Beat element" that places the Nuyorican performance style in the lineage of Kerouac, while also owing something to the poets' "street culture." Of all the poems featured in the film, these performances really do stand out; they're difficult to place properly, or pin down. There is an unbridled intensity to them, and a range of expressed, material concerns, that seem to demand a different level of engagement.

This section of the film closes with Piñero's performance of "Seekin' the Cause":

> . . . his voice still yellin' stars & stripes 4 ever
> riddled with the police bullets his taxes bought
> he died seekin' a Cause
> seekin' the Cause
> while the Cause was dyin' seekin' him
> he died yesterday
> he's dyin' today
> he's dead tomorrow
> died seekin' a Cause
> died seekin' the Cause
> & the Cause was in front of him
> & the Cause was in his skin
> & the Cause was in his speech

& the Cause was in his blood
but
he died seekin' the Cause . . .

What is invariably lost in the transfer from the live perfor-
mance stage to the pages of a trade paperback? The raw force
of delivery, of course, the intonation and sound of the poet's
voice, but also something far more intricate and elusive.
The spoken word poem begins long before the poet says a
single word: the poet's clothing, the look on her face, the
lingering trace of the last poem performed, or song played by
the band, before she steps in front of the microphone. The
audible sense of expectation in the crowd and their response
once the poem's final punchline falls flat, takes flight, or else
lands somewhere in the middle, but with just enough energy
to propel the work toward its triumphant conclusion. Call-
and-response does not live a full life on the printed page. We
can transfer the fact of its occurrence, and even create that
dynamic between a reader and written prose; but the feeling
of it in the densely packed café on a Wednesday night, or a
Loisaida living room in the summer when you reach out and
the gathered multitude who did not know your name once
but know it now, will always remember it, reaches back? The
page cannot entirely capture that on its own. The stage sets
it free.

Book 2:

THE BIRTH OF SLAM

This is for the lonely ones,
The older ones,
Passed on now
Silenced by speeding time
Less significant than once before
Beleaguered by the goals they did not
achieve.
Consumed by the failures haunting their
final hours,
The disappointments, the miscues, the
wrongheadedness,
The attachment to what never was or ever
would be.

This is for average folk manipulated by
desires
Sold to them from the first cry of birth—the
innocence of youth
Conditioned by institutions, religions,
governments,
Commerce, and misguided leaders of the
same.

This is for the heroic middle maintaining as
Best it can.

—Marc Smith

One myth is that all slam poetry is overtly political, loud, confrontational, or performed exclusively in the hip-hop idiom. Although such tones and language may be de rigueur at many slams, sometimes tiringly so, there exists a variety of poetry being practiced on the slam stage—comedic, dramatic, sensual, personal, and political. This is not to say that the slam community isn't a politically motivated one; slam poets and their audiences are by and large committed to celebrating ethnic, gender, and sexual diversity. But it is to say that there is more than one poetic approach used at the slam to state one's convictions. . . . The sheer variety of work performed in competitions signals that slam poetry—if we can think about it as a body of work—is not defined by tone, form, or subject matter, but by what it wishes to achieve: a more intimate and authentic connection with its audience through performance.

—Susan B. A. Somers-Willett

the greatest Americans / have not been born yet / they are waiting patiently / for the past to die.

—Saul Williams

Amethyst Rocks

Saul Williams was introduced to the underground poetry scene in New York in 1994. Williams, an aspiring actor, had just graduated from Morehouse College and journeyed to New York City to embark on the next stage of his adventure as a young artist: the beginning of his course of study in the MFA program in acting at NYU's Tisch School of the Arts. He was living in Brooklyn, and within weeks of his first encounter with spoken word at a local open mic, stumbled upon the Brooklyn Moon Cafe, on Fulton Street in Fort Greene. On his first evening there, he ended up meeting a coterie of poets and musicians that he would collaborate with for the rest of his career: Yasiin Bey (aka Mos Def), Jessica Care Moore, Asha Bandele, Talib Kweli, and Sapphire. All of them gathered there, in one room, that autumn and winter, and Saul watched one poet after another recite their work, thinking that the pacing, the content, the energy of these poems reminded him of the writings in the bedside journal back in his apartment, which he had never shared with anyone. He decided, then and there, that the next time he walked into one of these readings, he would get onstage and share, no matter what. Fast forward: spring break, 1995. Saul has a brief respite from his grueling rehearsal schedule at Tisch—eight hours a day, six days a week—for the academic holiday. He's been working on this one poem for a while, and he thinks it might almost be ready to share at the open mic. Its title is "Amethyst Rocks."

Saul returned to the Brooklyn Moon on March 16th. It wasn't a visit he had planned in advance. He was headed home that night, on his way back from the airport, from his spring break trip to Seattle. He noticed, looking across the street, that the windows of the Brooklyn Moon were fogged up, and naturally became curious about what was going on inside. He dropped his bags at home and walked over. It was an open mic not unlike the one he'd seen in the fall. All the heavy hitters were in the spot and had signed up to hit the stage: Jessica, Yasiin, Talib. Saul signed his name at the bottom of the page. He would be the last poet of the night to perform.

Williams recalls, in the course of his retelling, the more muted, somewhat nervous energy of the performances that night. It was a local open mic after all, and it featured mostly amateur poets, reading out of their notebooks, still finding their voices within the new work. Suddenly he realized that while inscribing his poem line by line into his journal, he had memorized it entirely. After the penultimate poet finished their reading, the open mic host for that night introduced him. He got up onstage, and the rest of his life began:

I stand on the corner of the block
slingin' Amethyst Rocks
Drinkin' 40's of mother earth's
private nectar stock dodging cops
Cause 5-0 be the 666
And I need a fix of that purple rain
The type of shit that drives membranes insane
Oh yeah I'm in the fast lane snorting candy yams

That free my body and soul and send me like Shazam
Never question who I am
God knows
And I know God personally
In fact he let's me call him me
Yea I'm serious B
Dogon niggas plotted shit lovely
But the feds is also plotting me
They're trying to imprison my astrology
Put our stars behind bars
Our stars and stripes
Using blood splattered banners as nationalist kites
But I control the wind that's why they call it the hawk
I am Horus son of Isis son of Osiris
Worshiped as Jesus resurrected
Like Lazarus
But you can call me Lazzy, lazy
Yeah I'm lazy cause I'd rather sit and build
Than work and plow a field
Worshiping a daily yield of cash green crops

Stealing us was the smartest thing they ever did
Too bad they don't teach the truth to their kids
Our influence on them is the reflection they see
When they look into their minstrel mirror
and talk about their culture
Their existence is that
of a schizophrenic vulture
Yea there's no repentance
They are bound to live

an infinite consecutive executive life sentence
So what are you bound to live nigga
So while you're out there serving the time
I'll be in sync with the sun
while you run from the moon
Life of the womb reflected by guns
worshiper of moons I am the sun
And we are public enemy number 1.[1]

Immediately following his performance, Williams was flooded with requests from the poets and audience members gathered in the venue that night. Suddenly, the entire world of New York City's Lower East Side poetry and performance scene opened up to him. "Someone came up to me and said, 'Hey, Allen Ginsberg's doing a reading at NYU. I'd like you to open up for him.' Someone else came up to me and said, 'The Last Poets and Gil Scott-Heron are doing something at the Wetlands. I'd like you to open up for them.' Someone else said, 'The Roots are performing at S.O.B.'s. I'd like you to open up for them.' Someone else said, 'KRS-One and the Fugees are performing at Rock Against Racism, and I'd like you to open up for them.' Someone else said, 'Amiri Baraka and Sonia Sanchez are performing at Medgar Evers College . . .'" It went on like that. And, he adds, "that was all one night. And I had one poem."

From then on, Williams started going to the open mic session at the Brooklyn Moon every Friday. From his vantage, he says—in no small part because he was so excited about what they were all doing—the environment wasn't competitive at all. More than anything else, what the collective of Brooklyn Moon poets had created felt to him like a dialogue they were all participating in about poetry itself: poetry both as a vehicle for larger ideas about human experience and also as an excuse to get together.

Williams, who grew up in Newburgh, New York, was the son of the Rev. Saul Williams, Sr., the pastor of Baptist Temple, Newburgh. He was a precocious child, who decided that he wanted to be an actor around the age of eight or nine. His father was opposed to this idea from the very start. Saul later clarified for me that, even then, there were older voices in the congregation saying he should follow in his father's steps as a minister. But those weren't his father's dreams for the boy, either. Instead, he wanted him to become a lawyer. His mother suggested a compromise.

"Ah, then you should do your next book report on Paul Robeson," she told him. For the rest of Williams's academic career, from elementary school up through his MFA training at Tisch, he would heed his mother's call. He wrote an essay on Robeson every year, each time focusing on a different aspect of the man's life. Robeson, of course, was an incomparable polymath: actor, singer, elite four-sport athlete in baseball, football, basketball, and track who eventually went on to play for two teams in the National Football League before earning his law degree from Columbia University, and becoming the world-famous performer and civil-rights advocate. One imagines that this reality lent a particular charge to a young Saul's decades-long biographical experiment, the gradual expansion of his knowledge of Robeson's life, at every turn, serving as a guide for his own radical aspirations. Williams's parents, in addition to being students of history, were avid theatergoers. Growing up, Saul saw everything playing both Off Broadway and on Broadway in New York City, a road trip that took about an hour and a half in either direction. It was the songs, specifically, of the Broadway stage that took hold of young Saul and wouldn't let go. Those musical performances were always there, at every step of his journey, fresh in his mind's eye and ear. This emphasis on music wasn't limited to the theater. In an oft-quoted piece of autobiography, Saul says that his mother was "rushed from a James Brown concert to give birth to [him]" in 1972. The poetics of protest, he seems to suggest, have been with him from the very beginning.

At the Baptist Temple, where his father preached, Saul would often see one of his neighbors, a man who sang what Williams remembers as "weird school songs" invited to the front of the sanctuary to share his music on Sunday mornings. That man's name was Pete Seeger. In his own words, Saul "grew up" with Seeger, "without really realizing everything that Pete Seeger had done." He recalls being surprised that his father, a black man leading a black church, would regularly invite Seeger to perform not only the "school songs" he remembers vividly, even classics like "If I Had a Hammer," but also songs like "We Shall Overcome," which Williams rightfully associated with the civil rights movement, without knowing at the time that Seeger had a role in writing the lyrics. Singers like Seeger, from across the spectrum of the American musical canon, would come and sing at Baptist Temple and stay at the Williamses' house up through Saul's teenage years. Music was an integral part of their family culture. He started writing rhymes when he was eight years old, and by the time the late 1980s arrived the practice of putting couplets together on the page was like breathing. Eventually, his interest turned more explicitly back toward the theater. He began to read Shakespeare's plays and poems in his spare time and write raps in Elizabethan English. When it came time for the cafeteria-table freestyle sessions that characterized that age for so many of us, Williams would ask his compatriots to stop banging on the table for a second so that he could recite his verses a cappella: "No beat, no beat—just listen."

Shakespeare wasn't the only writer a young Williams spent time with, however. He was well acquainted already with the works of Nikki Giovanni, Sonia Sanchez, Amiri Baraka. Their books had been gifts from his parents—gifts, he reflects, that he "took for granted at the time."

Now he'd come home to verse—to this space in the Brooklyn Moon where, in those days, it was possible to just try a bunch of different things out. All new material all the time, sharpening the fresh lines as part of an ensemble. Because Williams was still in graduate school at NYU for acting, he could only join up with the rest of the crew after play rehearsals, which he had just about every day. He would get out at eleven p.m., and then do whatever he wanted with the rest of his night. This meant that every time he stepped into the Brooklyn Moon, he was already coming from a performance space (and before that had spent ten or fifteen years of his life onstage). He already had a kind of facility in front of a room of strangers that was now bearing fruit in ways he never expected. Eventually, though, he found that in writing poems he could pursue an aim unavailable to him in his work as a stage actor. Since he was reciting his own work now, he was free to break the fourth wall, performing his own words as opposed to the words of a dead or living playwright. At long last, he was the author of the experience being shared. He could decide which way the story went, and precisely how it was told.

It was at this juncture of his journey, having been trained in the open, nurturing environment of the Brooklyn Moon Cafe and high-profile readings all around the city, that Williams discovered the competitive world of poetry slam. He had been at the café for a year or so when he first heard the term. His most vivid memory of it was a conversation between him and the poets Carl Hancock Rux, Jessica Care Moore, and muMs the Schemer during a regular Friday at the café as they were recounting a recent Wednesday night slam at the Nuyorican. When Saul initially asked what a "slam" was, exactly, no real explanation was offered other than "You should go, man. You should check it out." Once he got the crew to answer him, he couldn't believe what he was hearing. "I was actually disgusted by the idea of competing with poetry," Williams tells me. But his new friends and colleagues convinced him to come along, in no small part by telling him that past Nuyorican slam winners had gotten book deals and had recently published poetry collections. He was interested in that, and figured that if slam was a way there, he might as well give it a shot.

In March 1996, Saul entered the Nuyorican Poets Cafe for the first time. Little did he know that the Wednesday night he walked in was the last night of open competition before the beginning of the semifinals and finals for that year's Nuyorican Grand Slam Championship. Against all odds, with only the first poems he had ever written committed to memory, he won that night. He was asked—or, the way he puts it, "told"—to come back for the semifinals. He did, and won again. That April, only a month after his first time entering a slam, Saul Williams would become the seventh Nuyorican Grand Slam Champion in the venue's proud history.

*

Harold Bloom once stated in an interview with *The Paris Review* that poetry slam is "the death of art." I like that. The gravity of the statement feels like its own commendation. But I would like to offer here, perhaps as provocatively and along a different vector, that poetry slam is more accurately described as *the art of death*—the art of dying to oneself. You can hear the resonances of this approach in some of the descriptive terms of the slam itself, nowhere more vividly than in the role of the sacrificial poet: the first writer to touch stage during a slam. The work of the sacrificial poet is to perform just before the first competing poet of the first round, in order to "calibrate" the slam's five judges. These judges are chosen at random and can have no prior relationship to the poets involved, or even to one another. Each judge is asked to score participants' poems on a scale of zero to ten. The highest and lowest scores are dropped, and the average of the three remaining scores is announced as a poet's score for a given round. Thus, the highest score one can achieve is a thirty.* The order in which poets perform, what we call the "bout order," is determined by choosing numbers or letters from a hat, or bowl, or whatever other receptacle is on hand. Audience members show their approval of a performance by applauding (or snapping, or shouting the occasional "Amen") and their disapproval through booing, hissing, or even, in certain venues, the jangling of house keys.

Poetry slam is one of the few examples we have of a "language game" (to use Ludwig Wittgenstein's famous term, but not exactly the way he means it) that is explicitly named as such. One that is carried out in public, constantly, all around the globe. For Wittgenstein, a language game is implicit in our communication, and sometimes serves an explicitly pedagogical function. In *Philosophical Investigations*, he describes the term as referring to, for example, the way that a learner would learn to name objects: "that is, he utters the word when the teacher points to the stone" or, more simply, repeats a word after his teacher. Such simple operations, "by which children learn their native language," are what he calls language games.[2]

Slam, of course, is a language game in a different, though

---

* Thirty," it bears mentioning, can also be used a verb: e.g., "Last season, Matt thirtied every single time he competed." Matt is a person I just made up, but he is based on at least two people I knew for whom this was the case during a particular "slam season," i.e., the period of open competition in which one attempts to make a specific slam team, which will then prepare for a much larger, often national or international, slam that it will travel to as a representative unit.

related, sense. It is a place to play with words, and that is the entire point of the gathering: to think aloud under pressure and work out arguments in ensemble. It is a space where we craft a new order of symbols together: *time penalty* (points deducted for a poet going over three minutes), *indie* (a solo performance by a poet), *group piece* (a collaborative performance by two or more poets), *anchor* (the last poet you send up in a bout involving multiple slam teams), *leadoff* (the first poet you send up in a bout), *blocking* (the choreography behind a given poem)—an order that consists of words that sometimes have a related meaning in another context,* but once transferred to the world of slam take on new life, undeniable vibrance. Like most games, it can sometimes get out of hand in the high heat of competition. Like any game worth its salt, it is first and foremost a place to make friends. The language game of poetry slam, then, of the poetry slam scene, is one in which we are educating each other in another way that the social world all around us can sound, look, and feel. Collectively, the members of a scene are building their own world, pillar by pillar, stone by stone, wherein public acts of passionate utterance are not strange and unexpected but a natural part of the fabric of one's life, one's week, one's Wednesday and Friday nights now given over to raucous celebrations of the stories of strangers and friends, copious amounts of food and drink, dancing in the middle of the floor while late-nineties R&B falls like summertime rain over the room.

---

* "Anchor" and "leadoff," for example, both have clear antecedents in the world of track and field, while "blocking" has its roots in the world of theater.

Origin Stories

I competed in my first poetry slam back in 1999. I was eleven years old at the time. It was a Saturday afternoon, and I was with my mother in the Yonkers Public Library over by Getty Square, which I had only been to a few times, and knew best from the distant remove of my yellow school bus zooming past the building at three thirty p.m. each day. The library was located just across from the Hudson River. It was not too far from a small museum that bore its name (the Hudson River Museum), as well as a middle school named after the museum (the Museum Middle School), which has since been closed and is now named, in an interesting turn, for its proximity to the river (Riverside High School). The passage of years is strange that way. The carousel of names calls to mind one of my favorite lines from Susan Stewart: "Everyone knows that time is water / and, deeper, knows that water / erodes away all stone."[3] The flow of time is undefeated. The names on the buildings change, but the natural world wins out. The river stays the same.

I don't remember what my mother was reading. But she helped me whenever I had questions, even if only in the form of telling me to look something up on my own, or *think about it*, a classic refrain of hers that grated on my nerves for years ("I'm asking because the thinking isn't working!" I would say, visibly exasperated by the limits of my childhood cognition). After two or three hours at the table, we closed our books and headed downstairs to the lobby floor. I saw the stage with a microphone stand and flyer asking passersby to sign up for a "poetry slam" and thought little of it. I loved poetry, and had already been writing it for years, but had no idea what a slam was. Plus, I was ready to go home. The late morning and early afternoon spent studying had taken its toll. True to form, my mother had different plans. "Let's sign you up, Joshua."

I protested, of course. Not only because I was tired, but because I still didn't quite understand what I would be signing up for. "Slam" sounded like it involved wrestling of some sort, which I was a serious fan of at the time (D-Generation X and Mankind and The Rock in particular), if somewhat inadequately prepared to take up at that precise moment. But if a slam required *poems*, then I was in an even worse spot. I had none of my notebooks on me, and only one poem committed to memory at that point. Its title? "Hope and Love."* I thought the poem was fine—my seventh-grade English teacher, Ms. McCormick, seemed to like it—but it was in no way strong enough for something like this. There were already three rows of people seated in chairs across the library lobby for the competition. The sign-up list was full except for the last two or three slots. The lone microphone stand stood like a silver specter at center stage. I was frozen in place. "I know you can do it," Mom said. "I cannot," I clarified. "Gifts are meant to be shared," she said, in pretty much exactly those words, because that's how she talks. I had no retort ready for this unexpected gem. So I stared at the ground, searching for an answer that never came. I hung my head the entire walk

---

* I had not yet heard of the Jane Hirshfield poem by the same name, but I have grown to cherish it in the decades since.

over to the sign-up sheet, where I scrawled my name two lines from the bottom. I looked at the clock. We were a few minutes out from showtime.

The slam was hosted by a librarian, which made sense to me, even though none of the librarians I knew back then would ever let anyone be this loud in a library. By contrast, this host—let's call him Rob—encouraged the most raucous atmosphere possible: cheers of approval, applause, stomping and snaps, the entire gamut of effervescent praise. Then he explained the rules. This slam, unlike the standard I would grow accustomed to in the coming years, would have only two rounds. Eight of us had signed up in total. Four poets from that first group would move on to the second round, where they would recite another poem. The top three winners would be chosen from that second round of competition. My stress redoubled. The two-round structure meant that I couldn't perform the same poem twice. I whispered news of this unforeseen conflict to my mother, hoping we could leave the library on a technicality. Maybe stop by Carvel for ice cream on the way home. Pistachio for her, Rocky Road for me, as was our way. But instead of patting me on the head and ushering me outside, my mother assured me that I was mistaken; that I had overlooked something important. In one of the notebooks I brought to the library that day was a handful of poems I had scribbled in the margins during school. Whether she had somehow noticed this over the course of the day, or simply knew that my penchant for daydreaming and love of poems intersected in those middle-school spiral notebooks, I'm still unsure. But I went onstage with renewed confidence during the first round of the slam. We performed in sign-up order. The poet right before me was a man named Marcus, who had on a black durag, black pants, and black sweater. I remember his name because Marcus is also my brother-in-law's name, and 1999 was the year I met him, too. This other Marcus recited a poem that was electric, undeniable. It was about south Yonkers, and the violence that circumscribed everyday life there for people on the wrong side of generational poverty. He performed as if that poem was the most important thing he had ever written, or read aloud, in his life.

Saying that Marcus was a tough act to follow doesn't quite cut it. The performance was the most energetic recitation of a poem I had seen before. But there was no turning back now.

The host called my name. I walked up to the stage in the polo shirt and corduroys that back then were my daily uniform. "Hope and Love" was my first poem. It scored well, and I made it to the second round, where I competed against Marcus and an older gentleman who read his poems off a single piece of paper, freshly torn from his legal pad. For the second round, I went to the notebook and read with as much energy as I could muster. The entire crowd applauded, and the second poem scored about as high as the first. At slam's end, I took second place, and was awarded a small gold-plated trophy of a man with a torch in one hand and a scroll in the other. Marcus, who won the slam that day, told me that I had "heart." It was a piece of feedback I never forgot. I carried my trophy to the car and into the house later that afternoon, before placing it into the china closet: our family place of honor.

I now realize, for what feels like the first time but probably isn't, that I was the only child in the slam that day. My mother had signed me up to compete against adults, in a game I knew nothing about, simply because she knew how much I cared about the craft. Or perhaps, in stark contrast to the well-worn adage in slam that "the point isn't the points, the point is the poetry,"* my mother's aim in enlisting me for the competition that day had nothing at all to do with poems. I was terribly shy. I always had been. What I see now, much more clearly from the vantage of the future, is that getting me to read my poems—like getting me to act in plays, or recite Bible verses from memory in front of the sanctuary of our church—was about helping me practice not being afraid to speak *all of the time*. The "gift to be shared" my mother insisted upon was not only literary. There was something that's harder to pin down that she wanted me to believe in and develop: the sense that I was someone with a voice, with a vision and a critical worldview, and that these were not things to be kept to oneself forever. I could indeed be unafraid to be known. I could practice vulnerability in public and be met with something other than fear or malice. I could take that risk and come out on the other end alive.

Years later, this would be the essence of the pitch I made, as an arts educator, to parents unsure of how something like poetry slam could be of any benefit to the eventual lawyer or doctor they were raising, the child who, in their mind, had a future so far so from poetry in any form that slam, and spoken word by extension, was a waste of their time. "Slam

* This phrase was coined by poet and slam organizer Allan Woolf out of Asheville, North Carolina.

is a vehicle," I would tell them. The thing in and of itself has value, of course. But my sense has always been that the core competencies slam teaches—to memorize, to read text at the speed of everyday language, to speak with conviction and clarity in a brief window of time—are universally useful, no matter your field of endeavor or professional dreams. There are ongoing, irrevocable benefits to this craft, and to navigating the obstacles it presents in order to succeed. On that stage, for three minutes at a time, you can be whoever, whatever you want. That practice of everyday metamorphosis through embodied performance is a beautiful, necessary thing.

The poetry slam format has numerous origin stories and several historical antecedents that merit mentioning here. Many cultures across the globe have made use of literary events with a competitive element to achieve what would later be identified as poetry slam's central aims: first, to draw a crowd, and second, to provide a training ground for young artists to hone their craft. A renga, for instance, which has its roots in ancient Japan, was a long poem composed collectively in a contest atmosphere, with each poet in attendance adding lines in sequence, attempting to top the verse of their immediate predecessor. In Spain in the 1600s, hundreds of poets gathered in public to engage in poetry competitions called *justas literarias*.

Even in the twentieth century, there are direct antecedents to poetry slam that helpfully contextualize its influence and impact. In Chicago, the birthplace of the poetry slam format—the scoring, the judges chosen from the audience, the three rounds, the cash prize—there was already an ongoing series of poetry competitions sponsored by a man named Al Simmons, who created the World Poetry Association in the early 1980s. The WPA put on "poetry boxing matches" which took place in actual boxing rings, with timed rounds and the like. These Chicago bouts would eventually travel to New Mexico and be held at the Taos Poetry Circus, under the mantle of the Heavyweight Poetry Championships.[4] Famous winners of the competition included everyone from Ntozake Shange to Quincy Troupe (who won it twice), alongside any number of poets who blurred the boundary between stage and page and, what's more, showed skill as improvisers (there's a round in the Heavyweight Championships that requires this) that is worthy of admiration all on its own.

Which brings us to the period when poetry slam as we know it now was born: 1984–1986, the years during which a construction worker and avant-garde experimentalist named Marc Smith would get together on Monday nights with a group of friends, colleagues, and strangers at the Get Me High Lounge on Chicago's West Side, for a performance competition that inaugurated—but in some ways bears little resemblance to—what is now known across the world as poetry slam. Those nights at the Get Me High, for one, featured costumes and music and props, all of which are now explicitly banned for the most part in organized slam competitions across the country. There is little mention of anything like time penalties, for instance, which are now a crucial component of every level of slam, and regularly make the difference between who does and does not take home a win in an individual slam, even at the highest levels of competition. But the Get Me High Lounge was the first space that allowed Smith, a white, working-class writer in his late thirties, to consistently book whatever sort of performance work he wanted, including vaudeville, comedy, and more traditional poetry readings. Eventually he happened upon a format that seemed to resonate deeply with the crowd, which was a kind of mock poetry battle, wherein poets would have their work judged by strangers in the audience, first by jeering and applause, and then by scores. This early slam format stuck.

That initial group of writers at the Get Me High are referred to in the slam literature as both the Ill-Bred Poets of the Get Me High and, more formally, the Chicago Poetry Ensemble. The members of the group were Mike Barrett, Anna Brown, David Cooper, Ron Gillette, Jean Howard, Karen Nystrom, John Sheehan, and Rob Van Tuyle. These writers hailed from a truly eclectic range of fields: they were a copywriter for the *Chicago Tribune*, a performance artist, a paralegal, the editor of a floral magazine, a model, a student, a former priest, and a high school teacher. They were all over the map professionally, and gathered under the roof of the Get Me High to perform a poetry without discernible barriers or spatial limits. These were poems yelled from the top of the bar, or else out the back door, where a stranger walking down the street might hear it, without knowing its source.

At least at first. Because for those first two years, the Chicago Poetry Ensemble's Monday nights at the Get Me High were a wild success. So much so that Smith was eventually able to create a cabaret show called the Uptown Poetry Slam at the Green Mill Cocktail Lounge on Chicago's North Side, where he would debut the poetry slam format that we are now most familiar with. The Green Mill was purchased by a club owner named Dave Jemilo, who was familiar with the ensemble through their performances at another venue he owned in the city, the Deja Vu. When he purchased the bar in 1986, he thought they would be an ideal fit for Sunday nights, where the ensemble could host, on a weekly basis, the experimental new poetry show they had been working on. The Green Mill was where the term "poetry slam" was coined and its rules first devised, though the famous "So what!" response to Marc Smith introducing himself as host was a holdover from the Get Me High. There are a few competing theories about this tradition, why it matters, and why it persists. The first is that it was meant, from the very first, to be an act of self-effacement on the part of Smith. In his own words: "My So What! Handle came from the early days at the Get Me High Jazz Club when it was important to remind everybody taking the stage, including myself, that we were on equal footing with everyone else."[5] But there's an important irony here. By opening each slam this way—and baking this ritual into the way that so many other slams across the country begin—Smith also guaranteed his place in the lore and practice of the form. No matter where you are, every time there is a slam, there is a chance his name will be mentioned. He has, in his own way, guaranteed that his name, his contribution to an ancient practice of storytelling, lives on in his creation. Even when he is not present. In this sense, "So what!" cuts in multiple directions from the very start. It is both a refusal and a reminder. A monument in the form of embodied practice.

The first poetry slam on record took place on July 20, 1986. Though the competition was eventually the primary draw for local audiences, the Green Mill also featured plays, dance performances, and live music. It was, explicitly, a haven for all of the performing arts; not just poetry. In the beginning, in fact, the slam was simply added on as a kind of afterthought as the final set of the evening. It was the closing event of the night, and offered two distinct prizes: either ten dollars in cash, or several Twinkies (the Twinkies came first, and the money was viewed as a later upgrade).* Over the next four years, poetry slam spread its wings across the country, finding one of its most secure footholds at the Nuyorican, where Miguel Algarín and the other founders collaborated with the poet, curator, and eventual record label executive Bob Holman to create a slam of their own in the early 1990s, adding a new wrinkle into the format. As a result of a combination of slam victories on Wednesday and Friday nights throughout a given season, a poet would eventually be named the Nuyorican Grand Slam Champion (in those days, the title even came with a crown and purple cape). The first of these poets was chosen in 1990: Paul Beatty.

At this point in time, Beatty was only a few years into his journey as a poet, having just graduated with an MA in psychology from Boston University. While he was still in school, Beatty began to grow disenchanted with his strictly academic pursuits. One day, on a walk through a used-book store on Beacon Street, he stumbled across a poetry collection by E. E. Cummings, recalling the poet's noted habit of not using capital letters. This preference for eschewing

* The Twinkies story has been confirmed in multiple texts, often by Smith himself.

convention—especially in a moment where he was feeling constrained by the social codes of his graduate program—resonated with Beatty. It would come to be a hallmark of his style as a poet. As several of his friends from Boston headed off to join the Air Force, and he realized that he didn't want to enter the working world just yet (in psychology or otherwise), Beatty made a firm decision to switch gears. He began writing poems of his own, and eventually applied to the MFA program in creative writing at Brooklyn College. Beatty was admitted, and matriculated there in the fall.

To his surprise, what he found in the MFA program was a far cry from the sort of creative freedom he'd imagined when he made the decision to leave psychology for the literary arts. Here, he found the same unflinching dedication to specific forms and pedagogical approaches that had made him feel so stifled in the first place. He had been trying to escape the sense of being trapped within a given framework, feeling like a perpetual outsider. And now here he was, the only nonwhite person, not only in his cohort but in the entire program, constantly having to explain his language choices and reference points, while also experiencing moments of outright racial animus in workshops. And yet Beatty, somehow, pushed through. Even in the midst of so much difficulty, his skill set as a poet continued to grow and be recognized. In the words of one lecturer at Brooklyn College, Louis Asekoff: "He writes out of a web of life that doesn't look like allusions to you when you're using them. . . . I used to tell him that if any of his poems were anthologized fifty years from now, there'd be as many footnotes as T. S. Eliot's *The Waste Land*."[6] Beatty made his way to the Nuyorican after his last year in the

MFA program at Brooklyn. His style translated beautifully to the nascent slam scene there.

Having finally found his audience, Beatty would now be sent as the sole representative of the Cafe to the first-ever National Poetry Slam (which is often referred to via the shorthand "NPS"). At this inaugural slam, held in San Francisco, he would compete against full four-person teams from both Chicago and the Bay Area, whose team had been assembled by the poet and florist Gary Glazner. By all accounts, the first NPS on record was a success. Poets and audience members from across the Bay Area assembled at the Fort Mason Center for Arts & Culture, which boasts a gathering space of a little over fifty thousand square feet, room enough for a little under four thousand people to congregate at any given time. The first National Poetry Slam on record didn't do anything close to those numbers, but it wasn't a ghost town, either. As a matter of fact, according to Marc Smith's version of events, the evening was rather well attended. "About three hundred people showed up . . . quite a crowd for a poetry reading in those days. . . . Plopped down in the first rows with their arms crossed over their chests were more than a few sour faces ready to dismiss this 'slam thing' as just another desperate gimmick to con people into attending a reading by a group of aspiring nobodies." The "nobodies" in question, however, were undeniably successful at rousing the audience to their cause. "The team was comprised of Patricia Smith, Dean Hacker, Cin Salach, and me," writes Marc. "Patricia stepped to the microphone and by the time she finished the audience was on its feet roaring applause. Not a sour face could be seen anywhere."[7]

One of the major accomplishments of that moment—aside from the beautiful fact of all these different poets, who might otherwise have never met each other, sharing their work in the same place—was the awareness of a potential in the game that extended far beyond its city of origin: "Standing ovations cheered on the Chicago team for the rest of the evening. And the San Francisco team got their due, as well. The fire had been brought down from the mountain, and the room knew something important had just happened."[8] The Chicago team, according to Marc Smith, was showing the larger community that "what we had uncovered in Chicago and developed into the powerful performance style was a craft and a technique that they, too, could learn and apply to their performances and shows. Poetry no longer needed to be treated like a museum piece or school lesson. It was as dynamic and exciting as any of the other performing arts."[9] And so it was: the National Poetry Slam was born, and the planning began immediately for the following year.

*

Viewed through the lens of Marc Smith's vibrant myth-making, we discover the presence of a tension that persists even still. Here, at the event that serves in a sense as slam's arrival on the national stage, we hear in Smith's description a foundational, triangular relationship between three separate and possibly competing sites that could have a claim on spoken word poetry: the space of the slam itself (the bar, the local café, the community center), the marketplace (an ever-present threat to the sacredness of the art form), and the elite academy (whose exclusivity in some ways functions as slam's condition of emergence). Smith describes the liveness of slam, its inescapable energy, in direct opposition to the idea of poetry that might be encountered as a "museum piece" or a "school lesson." That is, poetry by dead people that deadens rooms, or else poetry that drains the life out of language, that de-emphasizes performance altogether, and does a disservice to its gathered audience by pretending they are not there at all. In his telling of what exactly took place at the first NPS on record, Smith makes clear that the poets gathered in the name of slam—and especially the Chicago poets, he is careful to point out—did not just inaugurate a self-contained competition; they showcased a model for literary community, and literary citizenship, for the rest of the world to follow.

When discussing another event altogether, a slam held during the third annual National Poetry Week Festival in 1990, Smith remarks that "the slams were getting a lot of media coverage; radio and even CNN picked it up and that of course stepped on the toes of the local poetry bigwigs." This element of competition within the competition is ubiquitous. Poetry slam is always the new kid on the block, in conflict with both a more plainly "literary" form of poetry that might challenge its rigor or aesthetic quality and even other forms of poetry competition, such as the Taos Poetry Circus. Gary Glazner, one of Smith's longtime collaborators, writes, "I got a loudspeaker permit and cruised the city with a carload of poets hyping the event. I spent one afternoon calling over 200 people in the National Poetry Week Festival Rolodex, putting over 100 people on the guest list. I hired Whitman McGowan to be a barker to stand out in front of the venue and call people in carnival-style." He recounts that it was at the first NPS in San Francisco, when he and Smith were together, that the latter suggested he might put on the event the following year. This was the beginning of "the comradely concept of passing the National Poetry Slam from city to city that continues to this day." In Glazner's words, "That idea drove the early growth of slam."[10] At the intersection of Smith and Glazner's accounts of slam's early days emerges a key point about the history of the form: the flair and flash of slam were always key components of the proceedings. It was always meant to serve as a way of approaching the presentation of art that centered on wildness, humor, and no small measure of occasional absurdity. Slam was never meant to be properly coiffed, codified, or contained. Even the basic rules were still in flux (again, it seems that there was little talk in those early days about time penalties, or a ban on props just yet). It was generally chaotic, barely subdued, and only just showing glimpses of what it would one day become.

The second NPS, in 1991, featured a widely expanded roster of poets and cities. The competition took place in Chicago over the course of four days and featured teams from not just the central triad of New York, Chicago, and San Francisco but from Ann Arbor, Boston, Cleveland, Milwaukee, and St. Louis as well. Patricia Smith was again the star of the event, taking home the individual poetry slam championship for the second year in a row: a title she would claim two more times in her career.

Like many poets of my generation, my introduction to Patricia Smith's work was some combination of YouTube videos and word of mouth, her reputation as one of the greatest poets in the history of slam already cemented by the time I discovered the form. For so many of us interested in the dance between page and stage, in making what at one point felt like a leap or a transition between genres, but which I now see more as an exercise in what a friend of mine once called "using all of your Englishes," Patricia's work was the bridge. When I was on tour at the beginning of graduate school, I carried her National Poetry Series–winning collection, *Teahouse of the Almighty*, with me everywhere. I studied its music that I might better comprehend my own. It was those lines—"And now this child with rusty knees / and mismatched shoes sees poetry as her scream / and asks me for the words to build her mother again"—that I used to better understand how the raucous sounds of the slams that had already shaped me might find a fitting home in the pages of a book.[11] Those train cars, buses, and plane cabins were my workshop, and Smith's work one of many instruments I would gather over time.

"How did I do this?" she said, repeating a version of my question back to me, when we talked about her early days in slam. "The first thing that happened was I found out about a program called Neutral Turf in Chicago in the late eighties. I think it was probably '87, '88. They put together this program that supposedly was going to bring together street poets and performance poets and academic poets." But Smith was less interested in categories of poets than in the characters inside her poems: "I get really invested in the people in the poems, and I think about them often. I wonder what happened to them. Even if it's not someone who actually exists. I never really drew those thick lines between genres." Smith also became a crime and mystery writer, and has written in other genres as well. "I had something I thought was a poem," she told me, "that was chosen for Best American Essays. It was a prose poem."

Even the language Smith uses to describe various divisions within poetry communities at that time—"performance poets" *and* "street poets," and both categories juxtaposed against poets from the academy—helps elucidate how each poet in the story of slam has their own way of resolving or approaching the tension Marc Smith mentions throughout his career, in print and elsewhere: i.e., between spoken word performers and "academic poets"—a conflict that is eventually mapped, at a different point in slam's history, onto the distinction between stage and page. In Patricia Smith's case, she showed us that there are writers for whom form is less a constraint, or a set of discursive and historical demands, than it is a range of tools.

For Smith, the borders not only between various fields or visions of poetry but indeed between reality and dreams *were actively blurred*. The people in the room and the people in their poems are suddenly one large chorus, worthy of our care and attention. To recite these stories out in the open air is enough, for Smith, to give them life. To name the character, the speaker, their beloved friends and local community, was also to animate something that must be accounted for, honored, and remembered, even once you leave the space. Such capacious, courageous thinking is a hallmark of Smith's writing across genres, and across time.

Promethean Fire

By the time the National Poetry Slam reached Boston in 1992, the roster had reached twelve teams in total, who were now performing before a live audience that numbered in the thousands. The year that Boston hosted NPS was a turning point for two primary reasons. First, it was the competition where the basic four-day layout of a national slam tournament became more or less the letter of the law. Second, and perhaps most importantly, the Boston slam represented the codification of the National Poetry Slam as a yearly meeting that passed, in Marc Smith's words, "like an Olympic torch" from city to city—picking up the Promethean metaphor from his description of Patricia Smith's performance at the first NPS in San Francisco.

In most written versions of the beginnings of slam—ranging from poetry anthologies to interviews and newspaper articles—it is positioned as an outlier within a much larger history of poetry competitions. The Taos Poetry Circus is perhaps the most useful example. Founded by Peter Rabbit (born Peter Douthit) in 1982, it is often positioned within the history of slam as a competitor that lost out in the natural evolution of performance poetry as a genre—simply one game among several that slam "shot past" on its way to mainstream cultural relevance.

But I wonder if there is another way to view its role in slam's history. As recently as a 2011 interview with the *Chicago Tribune*, Marc Smith says that the origin of the term "slam" was not (as I imagined when I was an adolescent) rooted in wrestling, but in baseball: "I was being interviewed by some reporter and asked what these things were called, and I had just been watching a baseball game and I was thinking . . . slam, grand slam . . . Poetry slam."[12] According to this account, then, slam was named in a moment of improvisation. And yet, if the foundational metaphor of poetry slam is not the body slam, not a collision between a combatant and the mat or the ground, but a grand slam, the contact between bat and ball and four runners coming back to home base, then what are we to make of the "bout" as slam's structuring, individual unit? This could, of course, be a case of a mixed metaphor that simply stuck around. What I think is more likely, though, is that the "bout" actually represents the encoded influence of the Taos Poetry Circus, and what its participants called their "Heavyweight Poetry Bouts." Rather than simply moving past its predecessor and competitor, then, slam incorporated some of its most compelling features and folded them into its approach.

The founder of Taos, Peter Rabbit, studied poetry at Black Mountain College with Charles Olson, an experimental poet and essayist who championed the organizing of poems by breath and ear, an innovation that feels right at home in the world of spoken word, though Olson is not commonly associated with it. In the very DNA, it seems, of these various forms of modern poetry competition is both the outspoken repudiation of certain forms of academic elitism or influence and a tie to various university spaces, to college students and the professoriate, that simply cannot be denied.

Several years after the founding of slam, in fact, in 1991, Marc Smith would go on to teach a poetry class at Lewis University outside Chicago. There he taught an undergraduate student named Mark Eleveld, who eventually became the editor of *The Spoken Word Revolution*, a 2007 anthology of poetry and essays that speaks to the larger influence of poetry slam in the classroom and beyond. I had the chance to interview Eleveld, who spoke about the way spoken word took hold at Lewis. "On campus, we had a coffeehouse, which was run by Brother Mark McVann, and it really was a showcase for music, mostly folk music, to be honest with you. There were national acts that were coming through Chicago, and because you could book it on a Thursday, at an off-price kind of thing, they would come through. It was curated in that fashion. But Mark very slowly started booking performance poets or poets you would see at the Green Mill or at the Blue Note or at Jimmy's and the Woodlawn Tap and these sorts of things. He would book them for the coffeehouse, and they would come and perform. And it was just revelatory and mind-blowing. I'd never seen anything like it and it was fantastic." Out of this coffeehouse scene, something crossed over. Brother McVann, Eleveld said, "talked the dean into letting Marc Smith teach a class, and it was a class that was based on performance."

The classroom that Eleveld goes on to describe, Smith's classroom, was not only unconventional, but truly electric. Rather than emphasize a workshop atmosphere rooted primarily in correction or critique, in honing various poems until they were stage-ready, Smith emphasized collectivity and *conviviality*, how spoken word could be used to build bridges between absolute strangers, and how an individual performer, in the most fundamental sense, was mostly a vessel for something much larger and more interesting. "Our final project was to get up onstage at the Green Mill on a Sunday and perform," Eleveld explained. "And then [Smith] would be giving us the chapbooks and the different CDs at the time, or audio tapes, of different poets that would come through, and different music. His teachings were really about cacophony and group pieces and decentralizing an ego presence onstage. The more cooperative, the more blocking that could go on, the more costumes that were involved, the more theatrical and bigger-than-life it could be, the better it was for Marc and for the experience." Eleveld, who is from Illinois originally, and was becoming in some ways, through these experiences, the arts educator, writer, and editor he is today, met a number of crucial interlocutors on the bridge Marc Smith built. "He wanted to marry the art of performance and writing together," Eleveld told me. "To be entertaining and serving an audience. . . . Patricia [Smith] would come all the time, and Chuck Perkins would come, and there's this whole cast of characters that became my friends and a group."

So, what began as a righteous critique of a certain detachment from an audience, from accountability to anyone who might listen to the lone writer onstage, ended up making its way back to the very university that served as one of its principal objects of critique. No longer, in this version of events, is Smith the perpetual avant-garde outsider; he was someone working to enact a vision of the university that was altogether different, something a bit less tame or preprofessional. This classroom was instead a kind of performance laboratory, a training ground for the wildness of slam, with a live introduction to the thing itself built in. The entire point was collaboration, not only between the enrolled students but between those gathered learners and the larger ensemble of poets Smith knew in the real world—Patricia Smith and Chuck Perkins and Bob Holman, among others. In this way, the college classroom was simply a link in a much larger chain of spaces, both underground and above it, united in the cause of dramatizing everyday life in poems.

Eleveld paints a stunning picture of the spoken word scene in Chicago at this time, one marked by various literary crossovers you might not expect. "You could go to a small area of Chicago and every night there'd be two or three different poetry things going on," he told me. "Regie Gibson was touring so much and working with so many different people, he did an adaptation of a Kurt Vonnegut short story at Steppenwolf [Theatre] and Kurt Vonnegut was in the audience." Eleveld remembered how that meeting turned into an endorsement for Gibson from Vonnegut, an established literary lion: "So Regie ran down to him and said, 'Hey, can you write me what you thought of the performance?' And that became the back of Regie's book. It was a letter from Kurt Vonnegut to Regie, which was cool." The response that Vonnegut wrote down that night—which is eventually, as Eleveld mentions here, reprinted on the back of Gibson's 2000 collection, *Storms Beneath the Skin*—feels especially fitting here: "You sing and chant for all of us. Nobody gets left out." These two sentences, and the moment that produced them, remind us that the boundaries between something like highbrow literary arts and spoken word were blurred even back then—if not always in a way that was visible on a larger scale at long-standing institutions, then at least in the actual rooms where the art was made. At the Green Mill, the Nuyorican, and elsewhere, all sorts of writers across the spectrum of literary fame were meeting one another, sharing new work, and having their sense of things transformed. It wasn't simply a matter of spoken word being commercialized by outside influence, or mainstream literary poets being crowded out by an emphasis on performance. Something much more intricate, with a much longer history, was at play. These quiet moments, like the one between Gibson and Vonnegut, these collaborations in the dark, have always been there.

Another budding talent who found his way to the art form through this Chicago scene was Tyehimba Jess, who was pursuing his undergraduate studies at the University of Chicago in the 1980s. Jess, born in Detroit, would become the author of *leadbelly* (2005) and the Pulitzer Prize–winning *Olio* (2016), an experimental tour de force composed of sonnets, hymns, and historical narrative. But back then, he had no interest in becoming a poet. He wanted to major in English and study the tradition from an academic's remove. But then he discovered, in his own words, that he "hated that" and decided instead to major in public policy studies, go into social services, and become a social worker. During that process, though, Jess tells me, there was a set of fortunate circumstances that interrupted his professional trajectory and ultimately turned him back toward poetry. One of them was meeting both Marc Smith and Patricia Smith through the local slam scene: "Patricia, I met her at the Green Mill. Her work translates from the page to the stage in a way that was very instructive for me. But I didn't start participating in poetry slam until 1999. I was on the Green Mill team. That

was a big advantage, you know, being in Chicago, at the epi-
center of slam. Being a part of the Green Mill thing."

For Jess, like so many others, the slam was a singular
training ground and space of meaning-making within his
career—as well as a connection to a much larger universe of
creative writing institutions in the city that helped shape him.
The slam, as Jess narrates it, was best conceived as simply
one dojo among many in which he honed his approach as a
young writer. He began with the open mic scene, pivoted to
slam, and then almost immediately returned to the world of
academia, where his love of performance was sharpened by
poet-professors who trained him in the full breadth of black
arts and letters. On this front, he elaborates a list of names
both new and familiar: Kent Foreman (whom the *Chicago
Tribune* once called "the elder statesman of spoken word"),
Oscar Brown Jr. (a singer, actor, and playwright, who now has
more than a dozen plays and as many albums to his credit),
and Regie Gibson. Jess ends the litany with the icon Gwen-
dolyn Brooks, who hosted a slam one night where Jess won a
hundred dollars in prize money.

The teachings of an unsung hero of African American
poetics, Sterling D. Plumpp, also had a lasting effect on Jess.
He took Professor Plumpp's class on black aesthetics and had
what he describes as a kind of gradual epiphany. Every class
he would look up and see this older black poet at the lectern
talking about books he had never heard of before, but now
knew he would need for the journey ahead. "This is the life,"
he realized. "This is what I want to be." Then he got ahold
of the books they were assigned in class, and realized that

what Sterling Plumpp had accomplished over the course of his career was to explore the history of the blues, the history of jazz, and the way that both have worked their way through the lives of individual musicians in the African American expressive tradition. He saw a radical black intellectual and poet who was also interested in the African American past and in turning the vernacular on its ear, so to speak. A guardian and a guide, committed to tracing our lineage through sound. This was the model that Jess would follow.

Outside of the classroom, there was also the Chicago State University Black Writers Conference, where Jess met other luminaries: Ntozake Shange, Terry McMillan, John Edgar Wideman, Sam Greenlee (who wrote *The Spook Who Sat by the Door*), Haki Madhubuti, Sonia Sanchez, Amiri Baraka. Once a year, this entire galaxy of black stars would congregate under one roof, and the young Jess would sneak in with a blank notebook, anxious to record any wisdom they had to share with those assembled. Then there was the Guild Literary Complex, a community-based literary-arts organization in Chicago led by poet and arts administrator Michael Warr during Jess's time there. The Guild was special for him, he says, because it was one of the few places in an incredibly segregated city where "everybody would meet and be on equal footing." On a given afternoon, he would go and sit quietly in the Complex, absorbing the art programming happening all around him, synthesizing that music, that language, into his own, increasingly undeniable voice. And there was the HotHouse, which sometimes collaborated with the Guild Complex on events. This was another public arts space where the true multicultural, multiracial character of the city could be seen for what it was, from Jess's perspective, unobscured by various forms of institutional gatekeeping.

It was a time, according to Jess, when there was a certain cohesion in the Chicago he knew, *a way of being together as a citywide scene*, that resonated deeply with him. These were spaces that "held it down for the entire city," as he puts it. Spaces that had room, necessarily, for a kind of rawness, or unfettered energy, that was key to his development as a poet in his late twenties. "Slam returned poetry to folks' natural voice," he says. "It let people know that the average schmo can come in off the street, go up there, and be appreciated. Or you would get booed off the stage. Anything was possible."

So What!

As for Marc Smith, given what he built with the early slam format and in his teaching at Lewis, there is a painful irony to the turn things have taken in recent years. In 2017, when Smith was featured at the College Unions Poetry Slam Invitational (CUPSI)—held that year on the campus of the University of Illinois Chicago, fewer than four miles from the Get Me High Lounge, where he'd pioneered slam—he was booed off the stage while performing as the featured poet for the evening. During his set, he got the chance to perform only a handful of his poems, one of which, "Old White Guy Whitey," was later described as a direct cause of the controversy that would follow. Here are a few lines from the poem's final stanza:

Old white guy whitey
A sugar cube in someone's joke
Responsible for a mountain of dark deeds
Different, I guess, from all the other colors

Much of the poem expounds upon the central conflict on display here. It is the story of a man—an older, white male writer specifically—without a clear sense of the future, or his place in it. Someone asked to withstand, from his vantage, wholly unmerited criticism. And not only critique, but a sort of active displacement from the cultural milieu, on the basis of factors he cannot control. At the core of the poem, it seems, alongside these more plainly stated elements, is an abiding loneliness. A sense that the world has left him behind and is moving, at ever-increasing speed, beyond his reach. Smith's performance was widely panned by poets in attendance as outdated, insensitive, and offensive. At an event—and, at this point in the trajectory of slam, within an entire genre—primarily associated with the stories of historically marginalized communities, such a poem, we can imagine, felt not only out of place, but like a critique of the day's proceedings. It wasn't so much that these were *anti-identity* poems, but rather that they offered a vision of identity poetics much closer to Smith's vision of the world: one that purported to eschew certain forms of race talk—all while still trafficking, it bears mentioning, in the language of whiteness—for a more deliberate emphasis on class. This argument, at the level of performance and otherwise, did not go over well that day.

During his reading, a wave of young poets walked out of the venue in protest, while another group walked toward

Smith with their arms held in the shape of an X. After this had gone on for several minutes, Smith responded to the students, asking, "Are you all done yet?" Their reply? A chorus of voices offering in return: "Are *you* done?"

What does it mean for the founder of poetry slam to be rejected so powerfully not only on this specific occasion, but on a regular basis throughout the country—that is, in the opening statement before every slam—as an aspect of the game itself? In this frame, the "So what!" of my young adulthood feels to me not so much like an outright castigation of Smith—not like the rejection of the founder of slam at CUPSI 2017—but rather a refusal of ownership as a meaningful category. In this sense and others, the constant, now institutionalized refrain of "So what!" is Janus-faced. Though Smith coined the term, and insisted upon its repetition, to remove himself from the center of the proceedings, its place in the ritual also means, necessarily, that he is present, in word if not in the flesh, whenever and wherever, a poetry slam takes place. The ritual keeps his name, his legacy, alive. It ensures his place in the future of the form.

The crowd's rejection not only of Smith, but supposedly of *what he represents*, is important here. How does this moment, like so many in the history of spoken word, function as both a cautionary tale and a larger metaphor? What does it teach us about the limits of the desire for a clean history, and about the making of individual people into certain kinds of representatives—for a cultural practice, for a region, for an art form—in the first place? ("Let me just say," Jess told me, "Marc Smith is an undersung and/or unsung hero of American poetics.") Though understandable criticisms of Smith and his poems abound—his decision to perform a poem like "Old White Guy Whitey," if nothing else, betrays a misunderstanding of both his audience and the larger occasion—this moment carries a larger, symbolic importance in the history of poetry slam. What drew many of those college students to the art of slam in the first place, one imagines, is not only an abiding love for the game, but a desire for community while attending educational institutions in which they might feel alienated from various forms of social life. You do not have to be an expert to enjoy slam. You do not have to be a seasoned poet to participate in it. This democratic impulse is built into the form and allows it to be used in wildly different social settings and toward various, divergent social and political ends, any number of which Marc Smith himself could not have anticipated in the early 1980s, trying out a new bar game with his friends.

In that moment, these students—many of them taught by the very same sort of professors that Smith had repeatedly named as the erudite voices against which slam was established—turned a version of his own longstanding argument against him. Some were upset that, as Patricia Smith put it to me, "there's some white man named Marc Smith claiming he invented the slam." She continues, "I had to say, 'Okay, but back up, children. He did. He really did. We were there.'" As much as Marc had once claimed that poetry did not belong to the academic types, the professors and MFA poets, these young adults were now saying that the space at UIC *was no longer his to hold.*

As those closest to Marc Smith tell it, this event represented something of a major change for the man himself, and for the future of poetry slam at the Green Mill. Mark Eleveld told me that instead of the slam's classic setup, a raucous seven-to-ten set on Friday nights, it's now a bit tamer, three p.m., show for a somewhat different audience than usual. Patricia, in her now-classic essay "The Second Throat," reflected:

> Marc was just enough of all of us—a heartbroken souse, madly in love with lyric and leaving shards of his self-esteem on beer-slick floors. We appreciated his litany of failures and trusted him with our collective voice, trusted him to wail the stories we were afraid of. . . . Behind the mic, he wore our fears proudly. The stifled halls of academia wouldn't have had a clue about how to handle him. His words flowed like barroom light through a crack in a wooden door; he needed fools like us to cheer him on, and we needed him to trumpet the syllables we wouldn't dare. No one—no one—could have done this but him. He would be vilified, under-estimated, misunderstood, and attacked. He would be blamed for both his successes and his failures. His fiery poetics would be dismissed as mere snippets of theater, and the kingdom he had crafted would be pointed to as an example of what poetry can be if the unwashed, untrained, and underfunded get ahold of it.

Depending on who you ask, then, Marc Smith is a figure that takes on a myriad of forms: innovator, appropriator, inventor, altruist, teacher, friend. This range of readings is in some ways inevitable given the sheer breadth of his influence, acknowledged and otherwise. But it is also, I think, a useful metonym for slam itself. It is many things to many people: the death of art or a whole new life, commodified mass culture export or avant-garde detonation, exclusionary scene or haven for the most vulnerable among us.

Cheerful Anarchy

At CUPSI 2007, held at Eastern Michigan University, the host of our first bout was Lauren Whitehead. She shared a powerful poem before the announcement of scores, and I would later learn that she was helping coach that year's team from the University of Michigan, whom we would face in the finals. Lauren, who grew up in Chicago, is now a poet, playwright, and professor of dramaturgy at NYU. When I asked her recently how she found her way to spoken word, she told me, "Marc Smith came to my high school. He came to my high school, and he performed a poem. I remember seeing that—it was either my junior or senior year—and egging on one of my friends who I knew wrote poems, 'baby, get up and read a poem onstage!' Neither one of us felt brave enough to do it. That's the first time I ever saw somebody read poetry out loud, and I hadn't connected it to a larger movement in any kind of way."

Though neither Lauren nor her friend performed that day, the visit from Smith, and the introduction to the art of spoken word, had an indelible effect on the seventeen-year-old—one that she would not fully understand until the next year, 2001, when she matriculated as a freshman at the University of Michigan at Ann Arbor. While walking through the student activity center on campus, she overheard a loud voice reciting something she could barely make out, in a cadence that she recognized. She followed the voice to an open door. Inside were a group of students, around her age as far as she could tell, reading poems. Something immediately clicked for her. She had, of course, seen this before, back during that high school assembly in Chicago. She remembered her desire to go onstage, and her decision to stay seated. This time, she would make a different choice.

Lauren walked through the door and watched the young people perform. She saw a poet, Molly Raynor, read a poem about teaching and was moved to tears. Afterwards, she approached Raynor to ask for more details about the purpose of this strange, wonderful gathering, teenagers reading poems against the din of a dining hall and hundreds of students in transit. "This is a thing we do," Raynor replied, "It's called the Volume Youth Poetry Project." As Whitehead would soon discover, this program had no direct connection to the university itself, but was rather a weekly poetry workshop for young people put on by Neutral Zone, a teen-driven— and teen-founded—literary arts organization in Ann Arbor. Through her new relationship with Molly, Lauren was connected to the town's spoken word scene, and to the slam scene at the university. She says, "It was with Molly that I crafted my first spoken-word poem, and performed it at the union at the University of Michigan, and subsequently made my first slam. It was also through Molly that I understood that there was an adult poetry scene. Ann Arbor had an adult slam team, too. It was through that experience of meeting her at that poetry event that she was doing, that opened my eyes up to all three levels of the slam community, the youth, the college, and the adult."

Whitehead would eventually make Michigan's slam team and become a fixture on the squad during its run in the early 2000s. It was also during this period that she began working with high school students through Volume. During her sophomore and junior years, she would meet several other poets who remained friends throughout the years: Daveed Diggs, Rafael Casal, Chinaka Hodge—all of whom, like Whitehead, Saul Williams, and so many others, eventually made the leap into other genres. "In some ways that happened because the place where we started had this extreme boundary," says Whitehead. "We had three minutes, with a ten-second grace period. No more than four people, you couldn't do things with the microphone. No props. Very strict rules." She reflects on how these boundaries, by their nature, encouraged opposition—igniting their thinking about the possibility of stretching beyond, of "leaving the boundaries of a single body on a single stage with a single mic, to be in a theatrical space." She goes on: "I think many of us were like, 'Slam is so cool, language play is so cool and so fun, but we're outgrowing the boundary.' She mentions *Blindspotting*, a recent film written by Casal and Diggs, and adds, "That's why you get, like, a Chinaka Hodge album, MC'ing in a way that's still very reminiscent of slam, that still has all that stuff inside of it, but has really moved beyond that."

—

This urge to go *beyond the boundary*, to experiment with other genres while maintaining the core elements of a spoken word toolkit was also part and parcel of Whitehead's approach to adapting Ta-Nehisi Coates's memoir *Between the World and Me* for the stage of the Apollo Theater in 2018. "It's not surprising to me that when I am asked to do this thing with *Between the World and Me,* that my instinct on how to transform that thing goes back to my poetry tools. That's where I learned how to understand language, that's how I learned how to play with it. To make something that's a single narrative by one man to one other young man, to make that open enough for . . . it's almost counterintuitive, but to make it open enough for more people, you had to reduce it." There was a poetic distillation that Whitehead relied on to reach the emotional core of Coates's work. "There's a voice of rage. There's a voice of sorrow. There's a voice of romance. Rage, romance, sorrow, and the others become characters. Once you name that character, it's easier to shape the text that's already there."

Whitehead describes the movement from spoken word to other genres not so much as a departure but, rather, as an act of poiesis, as a making, or expansion: "All the tools we have to create character in some ways come from our understanding of poetry slam. It feels so much like home, and also like we've built bigger homes for ourselves."

Both Whitehead's stage adaptation of 2018 and the film *Between the World and Me* make use of the aesthetic sensibilities of spoken word; the 2020 film also features a cast of contributors who themselves have a deep connection to the more recent history of the art form, as well as its manifestation in the world of the dramatic arts and the contemporary landscape of American arts education. As part of an ensemble cast featuring voices as varied as Oprah Winfrey and Mahershala Ali and Tariq Trotter (better known as Black Thought of the Roots fame), Marc Bamuthi Joseph—the founding program director at Youth Speaks before taking on his present role as vice president and artistic director of social impact at the Kennedy Center in Washington DC—stands out, lifting Coates's words from the printed page with undeniable power.

In the film, Joseph performs in front of a vintage Unidyne microphone, one held within the exact same black microphone stand you would see at any number of poetry slams across the country. His pacing is swift. His hands fly back and forth in front of the mic, adding another layer to the picture his words are painting for the audience. There is no mistaking the source material. This is a clear nod to the poets everywhere who made this occasion possible: the decades of open mic and poetry slam performances that come alive through Joseph's voice and gestures, a kind of living palimpsest to remind us how we arrived at this moment. At its core, the film is a choral poem, composed of men and women and children from across the black diaspora. There are scenes of schools, parks, protests, family photos: iconic images of African American history and much more personal ones taken from Coates's family archive. In an especially memorable moment, the narrator proclaims: "I saw everything I knew of my black self multiplied into endless variations." And the film accomplishes just that: blackness expressed in seemingly infinite permutations; in every color, and voice, and genre.

Poetry is central to that expression. Mahershala Ali—in what is perhaps the most memorable monologue in a film filled with knockout performances—describes the first time Coates's speaker falls in love: "In my small apartment, she kissed me and the ground opened up. How many awful poems did I write about her?" And then there is Coates's reflection on the state-sanctioned killing of his friend and Howard classmate Prince Jones at the hands of the Prince George's County (Maryland) Police Department: "[These were] the same police that the DC poets warned me of." Coates calls on us to recognize an ongoing state of emergency that demands new language, new poetics, another way for us to tell the story of how we made it through. As was the case with the memoir, the film version of *Between the World and Me* centers on some of the most pressing social, political, and philosophical questions of our age: How will we respond to the ongoing catastrophe of anti-black violence in America? What will the unabridged truth cost us? At what point will this country take care of its children? The writing and performance of poetry was, in Coates's case, as it would be for many others, the laboratory for the exploration and expression of these urgent questions. In an April 2022 *Interview* magazine conversation between Coates and the MC Earl Sweatshirt—son of the late South African poet laureate Keorapetse Kgositsile and the legal theorist and black studies luminary Cheryl Harris—he talks a bit about his relationship to poetry: "When I was younger, I thought I was going to be a poet, and I used to read your dad . . . when I was at Howard. He was one of the Black Arts Movement guys that I studied."[13]

Coates, the son of a teacher, Cheryl Lynn Waters, and a publisher, W. Paul Coates, also studied the poetics of what was known as the "U Street scene" around Howard University in the early 1990s—a network of venues and cultural institutions (It's Your Mug, the Black Cat, Bar Nun, to name a few) that helped shape the writing of a generation of DC poets and performers. The scene was a mélange of live music (go-go, hip-hop, R&B) and spoken word styles forged from a collision of the black experimentalist tradition in DC and the spoken word aesthetics starting to spread around the nation from New York, Chicago, and elsewhere. In sum: Coates had a poetry education before he became the journalist and prose stylist in multiple genres that we know him as today. The adaptation of his memoir into a poem, and a play, and a film, feels like a fitting homage to that history.

The Champions

When the Nuyorican Poets Cafe adopted the slam format in 1990, the gatherings were wildly different from those once held in Algarín's living room. Now, fifteen years after its birth, the Nuyo was a space not only for the sharing of new work and the building of bridges, but for competition and the consistent, hungry audiences that high-stakes competition tends to produce. Surprisingly, many of the members of the original collective were quite open to the newfound popularity and shifting demographics of the Nuyo. The increasingly overflowing audience came with various benefits. The venue's popularity eased some of the pressure on Algarín himself to pour his own resources into it. New faces meant new income, and new income meant that the sort of community work the collective had prized from the very beginning—that is, the creation of alternative spaces for writers from historically marginalized groups of all sorts—would continue into the foreseeable future. Algarín understood, fundamentally, that there were people who came out for slams who might not come out to readings. But the slam wasn't about expertise or literary celebrity. At root, there was simply something magnetic about the idea of so many vibrant live performances under one roof. Every week a group of novices would get up and expound upon a range of topics, often with a sense of humor or righteous rage that was downright cathartic. It wasn't always about the individual person, or how incredible of a writer they might be. People went to the Nuyorican to feel something undeniable. Yes, they trusted the name of the place to draw some of the best young talent from across the city, but ultimately the point was just to be in the house, to give yourself a chance to say you were there when the magic happened. From the very beginning, the Nuyorican was one of the most exciting, best-known poetry slam scenes in the country, in no small part because of the range of poets who made their names there. Many of the Nuyo's first "Grand Slam Champions"—poets who won both a Wednesday- and a Friday-night slam during the season, in addition to the Grand Slam Finale in April—went on to great success as writers and performers outside the realm of slam. Along with Paul Beatty (now a Man Booker Prize–winning novelist and Columbia University professor), these include Daniel Beaty

(*Def Poetry* alumnus, actor, and dramaturg), Mayda Del Valle (award-winning performance poet and arts educator), and, of course, Saul Williams.

As we left him, on the strength of his very first public poem, Saul Williams had just won that Grand Slam Championship at the Nuyo. Two other major events in Saul's life took place that same night in April 1996. The first was that he met a man named Marc Levin, a film director. Levin told Saul that he was so moved by his performance that he would like for him to cowrite a film he was working on at the time: *Slam*. Naturally, Saul told Marc that he was in the process of getting his MFA in acting from NYU, and thus knew a great deal about acting but not so much about screenwriting. Marc had previously cast another actor, Bönz Malone, in the lead role, but Malone had been incarcerated earlier that month. After his conversation with Saul, Marc reached out to Malone to tell him he'd seen the young poet perform and was interested in having him star in the film in Malone's absence. What Marc didn't know was that Bönz was already familiar with Saul. He had seen him recite at a reading downtown and been thoroughly impressed. His reaction was immediate: "That dude? You got to cast him. He's the one." With Malone now onboard, Marc came back and asked Saul to both co-star in and co-write *Slam* with Sonja Sohn. He agreed. The script became a part of his MFA thesis at NYU.

Alongside this dream, Saul pursued another: that of writing his first book. A few months after winning the Nuyorican Grand Slam Championship, he would get his chance. Apparently, a reporter from *The New York Times* had gone to the slam on Friday night. Williams woke up on Septmeber 29 to see one of his poems on the front page of the paper. He was twenty-four years old. That day, he received a dozen calls from literary agents and speaker bureaus asking to represent his interests. Williams signed with an agent, who soon admitted (surprise of the century) that he wasn't sure he could get him a lucrative deal for his debut poetry collection. Given that this was the case, Williams decided to take up an offer from his friend and teammate Jessica Care Moore to publish his first book on her new imprint: Moore Black Press. Two years later, *Slam* debuted, and Williams was invited to Sundance. The film went on to win both the Grand Jury Prize for a dramatic film at Sundance and the Caméra d'Or at the Cannes Film Festival.

Suddenly, his agent's phone wouldn't stop ringing. He had book offers from Norton and Simon & Schuster. Enter Rick Rubin. Who, only days after Saul receives the news about the book offers, will hear one of the twelve-inch records that Saul previously recorded for Ninja Tune at a Tower Records ("or something," Williams clarifies), and reach out to his manager to work with him. It was in this sequence that, even before *Slam* was ever released to a mainstream audience, Saul ended up accepting both a book deal—he signed with Simon & Schuster—and a record deal, with Rubin's label, American Recordings. He put together a band and started performing regularly at CBGB and other venues around New York City, adding a punk rock sound to the spoken word aesthetic he had already mastered: "I'm basically in the mindset of 'If I have a platform, I feel as if we're living in a state of emergency. I cannot waste one word with ego play.' That was pretty much my MO at that time. I even turned down doing theater, and I'm fresh out of theater school. I turned down doing theater at that time because I felt theater is a delicacy. It's only reaching the elite." Saul remembers that this newfound stance was profoundly influenced by the social and political atmosphere around him at the time. "Maybe around the time Amadou Diallo was killed. I guess my upbringing had me in this mindset of . . . I need to say this shit right now, out loud, on the largest platform ever.'"

Williams turned down the Norton book deal and went with Simon & Schuster primarily, he says, because of their MTV Books imprint, which promised to make music videos for his poems. He recounts the meeting with MTV, where representatives from the imprint said outright that they had never worked with a poet before. They had only, to that point, published books related to MTV properties—*The Real World*, for example—but now felt a new level of social responsibility: "'We feel like we owe it to society because we feel like we played a role in diminishing the attention span of this generation.' They literally said that in the meeting," Saul tells me. "'And so, we're very interested in investing in poetry.'" The pitch resonated with him, and, after his debut collection, *The Seventh Octave*, which he published with Moore Black, he ended up publishing his subsequent three books—*She*, *The Dead Emcee Scrolls*, and *Said the Shotgun to the Head*— with MTV Books.

Williams starred in a second film in 1997: the documentary *SlamNation*, which followed the trials and tribulations of the Nuyorican Poetry Slam team as they traveled to compete in the 1996 National Poetry Slam. *SlamNation*, directed by Paul Devlin—another person Saul met that first night he competed at the Nuyo—went on to positive critical reception (Roger Ebert wrote a glowing review in which he described poetry slam as "cheerful anarchy") and had a major influence on the development of poetry slam scenes across the country. It served as both an advertisement for the National Poetry Slam itself, as well as the standard by which poets across the country could measure their proficiency as writers and performers. For countless audience members, *SlamNation* was an introduction to poetry slam as a competition and to spoken word as such.

SlamNation featured performances from contemporary writers such as Patricia Smith, muMs the Schemer, and Taylor Mali. Over time, it has become a fascinating historical object, a front-row seat at the beginnings of these poets' careers. Almost all of them have since pursued a professional direction that is connected to, but ultimately divergent from, poetry slam itself. Williams is now best known as a musician, author, and live performer; Smith is the author of seven books of poetry, including 2017's *Incendiary Art* (winner of an NAACP Image Award and the Kingsley Tufts Poetry Award and a finalist for the Pulitzer Prize), and the 2021 recipient of the Ruth Lilly Poetry Prize; muMs, who died in March 2021, became an actor and appeared in a recurring role on HBO's hit show *Oz* (fittingly, as a character named Arnold "Poet" Jackson) in addition to his work as a theater artist. *SlamNation*, in this sense, chronicled the earliest moments of an art form that would become a starting point for many writers, performers, and public figures in the years to come.

Works like the documentary, Tyehimba Jess remembers, also revealed both the best aspects of slam and some of its pitfalls. "When it arrived in the mid-eighties, the feeling was that poetry had gotten trapped in academia. It was trapped in the idea that someone needed a BA or a PhD in order to understand a poem." Slam was an outlet that helped complicate, and ultimately unmoor, this vision. But, he adds, the competition also had its various pitfalls. "If you watch *SlamNation*, you'll see what I mean. . . . Taylor Mali is in there. And he's formulating, over the course of that film, how to win the slam. It became formulaic in a certain kind of way." Here we see the ultimate utopian striving of slam—the return of poetry to something like a natural voice, the strange, tenacious music of the everyday—and the downside of its nature as a form of competition *as a game that can be gamed.* Even still, Jess adds, "The good thing about slam is you get critiqued . . . you start to understand what it means to have a serious level of dialogue with a live audience. And then you learn from that."

The television series *Def Poetry*, which premiered in 2002 and ran for six seasons, is another important example of slam training the voices of young writers all around us, as the competitions moved from the performance stage to the screen. As teenage poets, my friends and I all watched old clips of the show on YouTube, or else live on HBO at our cousins' apartments, the ones who had premium cable and were allowed to stay up late enough on a weeknight to watch. From the very beginning, the program dared to feature poets from every corner of the literary universe: Staceyann Chin, Shihan, Black Ice, Sunni Patterson, Beau Sia, Nikki Giovanni,

DMX, Ursula Rucker, George Watsky (a friend of mine from the youth slam circuit), and countless other poets appeared on the program and delivered legendary performances. In 2001, a number of these poets had their work anthologized in *Bum Rush the Page: A Def Poetry Jam*, which was edited by Tony Medina and Louis Reyes Rivera, and featured a foreword by Sonia Sanchez. In its five years on the air, *Def Poetry* further clarified for us all that there was an undeniable connection between this seemingly niche art form and the hiphop culture that had already taken over the world. The stage play that emerged from the television program, *Def Poetry Jam*, enjoyed a six-month run on Broadway and won a Tony Award for Best Special Theatrical Event.

*

After moving to LA in 1999, Williams began taking meetings around the town, talking to studio heads about potential roles. The lack of imagination he heard in those meetings was frustrating for the young artist; just about every part he was offered throughout this period was to play a police officer or a drug dealer. During those conversations, it dawned on him that he didn't actually need the support of mainstream Hollywood, though that was one of the professional paths he had been trained to pursue. He was already performing at colleges, writing new lyrics, recording. He was feeding himself with his original work. He could write his own way back onto the screen if he so desired. He didn't have to sacrifice his creative vision for a paycheck.

It was also around this time that Williams first started calling himself a poet. He had been hesitant to self-identify this way because he hadn't studied the craft of writing poems in school, and had no outside formal training, either. But it was in this period, when the books were coming out, that he made the conscious decision, over and against the draw of Hollywood, to invest in the literary arts full-time. The ancient moniker of poet finally felt like it fit. Indeed, it was this more long-standing sense of performance as a site of spiritual knowledge and power that began resonating with Williams as he went out on tour with his first full-length album with Rick Rubin, 2001's *Amethyst Rock Star*. He looked at every performance as a kind of ceremony. He would take off his shoes, sage the stage, and center himself. It brought him back to those days performing in the theater—moments, he says, "when the man I knew as Saul Williams would black out," when whatever worries he had before he stepped onto that stage would disappear, whatever notes, whatever blocking or feedback, and he would lose himself completely in the consciousness of a new character, uniquely prepared for the occasion. His goal, with the poems and the songs alike, was to achieve that level of immersion.

The Nuyorican remained one of the spaces where that sort of transformation was possible. The allure of the café at the time was due in part to the work of the poet Bob Holman, one of its most vocal supporters when the space first reopened in the wake of Miguel Piñero's passing in 1988. Holman was a fixture on the Lower East Side scene at the time, and would serve as the host of the Nuyorican's weekly slams from 1992 to 1996. In Miguel Algarín's own words, it was Bob who suggested the café reopen:

Holman approached me and said "Miguel, it's time to reopen the Cafe. This is the moment, you know, and Miky is insisting on it, and we are ready. Let's move on it, let's open the Nuyorican Poets Cafe again." Bob Holman's words later began to unravel a need that had been lying dormant in me ever since I had closed the doors of the Cafe for what had become a prolonged period. Yes, Miky's death was to be a new beginning. From the ashes, life. From the whispered promise made by one peer to another, the oral tradition was to find a permanent home at the Nuyorican Poets Cafe.[14]

It was also, in fact, Holman who brought the poetry slam over from Chicago to the Nuyorican during this period, a major step toward building the space that Allen Ginsberg would one day call "the most integrated place in the world." Holman, who was born in LaFollette, Tennessee, but grew up in a series of small midwestern towns, was drawn to storytelling and reading from a young age. When I speak with him for the first time, in fact, our conversation begins with the question of literacy. How and when we learned to read words on the printed page, and first began to link that newfound insight to the love of performance; to the feeling that it is and has always been an indelible part of us, there from the very beginning, helping shape the tenor of our lives. "I was refused admission to the upper echelon of eight-year-old reading when I was six years old and you were supposed to stay in your zone," he says. But he wanted to go, always, outside of the prescribed territory. He recalls choosing *Catcher in the Rye* for his end-of-year book report—a book that wasn't allowed in the school library: "My teacher refused to read it because of the filthy language in it." He found another teacher who was willing to read the report and grade his paper. "I think the poets a lot of times are just able to do things because they're on the fringes," he says. This is a recurring theme for Holman during our conversation: the study and pursuit of the kind of life that is only possible at the periphery, outside the bounds of dominant protocols for writing, speaking, getting together. It is in those rooms, Holman seems to suggest, in those bars and jazz clubs and cafes—or else outside, on the block, altogether disinterested in what's happening in the building—that he has always found his truest friends. Wherever that space is in a given moment, that's where the poets are gathering.

Holman's first encounter with the Nuyorican poets was several years after his time as an undergraduate at Columbia University. It was a moment of overhearing an unfamiliar voice and being struck by its power. He was still a young writer from the Midwest "falling in love with everything that the city is. But I also came here with a copy of *Howl* in my back pocket, and at Columbia [I was] studying with Kenneth Koch"—a witty, irreverent poet of the New York School, which also included Frank O'Hara, John Ashbery, and James Schuyler. Koch was a dynamo. "He walks into the room on the first day and throws his arms around himself, and he says, 'Oh, Walt, I love you.' And we were going to have a class on Walt Whitman, and I had never in my life heard somebody really talk to a dead poet in front of me, let alone using his first name when he talked to him."

Being at Columbia, Holman says, was a transformative

experience. Studying there in the late sixties helped, funda-
mentally, to place him within a tradition he once only under-
stood in the abstract. The poets, dead and alive, that Kenneth
Koch summoned in that class became real to a young Hol-
man. They too, in a sense, were his teachers. They instructed
him in their ways and gave him real models to aspire toward.
But this was only one element of the poetry education Hol-
man received during his time at Columbia. There was also
the opportunity to meet other living, breathing poets: to
read their books and share space at various venues across the
city. Koch was on a first-name basis with all the key poets,
Holman says. "Ginsberg was there, and Ashbery was there,
and [Gregory] Corso was there, and John Hollander was
also there, but mainly what was there was poetry itself and a
firsthand connection with it. And it was just like everything
that New York could offer. So I bought, at the Columbia
bookstore, *De Mayor of Harlem* by David Henderson. And
I got *Snaps* by Victor Hernandez Cruz, both of whom I
began becoming really close to, which shows you, I think,
what a tiny town Poetry is." Holman saw poetry as, in large
part, a social space. "All the poets of this scene were at the
party. How do you know you're in the scene? You're at the
parties."

From 1977 to 1984, Holman coordinated the readings
at the St. Marks Poetry Project. While listening to WBAI
one day—a freeform Pacifica radio station in New York—he
heard a voice that was quite distinct from the poets he'd lis-
tened to during his time at Columbia, or the years shortly
thereafter. The show he overheard that day, which had gotten
its start only a year before the beginning of his tenure at St.

Marks, was "Live from the Nuyorican Poets Café." "I had moved down to the Lower East Side, finally moved down from the Upper West where Columbia is, and heard this on the radio. It was a party that I had not been invited to, but they were saying come on down. And they were reading poems." In 1978, Holman would find himself onstage at the Nuyorican—backup band behind him—for the first time.

Though Kenneth Koch was a great teacher and poet, and Allen Ginsberg helped liberate his mind about poetry as performance—this is the same man who, Holman reminds me, once sat on the steps of William Carlos Williams, another great poet of Puerto Rican heritage, in New Jersey, until Williams agreed to write the introduction to *Howl*—neither of those writers, none of his great heroes, was connected to the culture of the street, of the moment, in the way that the Nuyorican poets were. They had their own world, and had no need, as far as he could tell, for the social scene he entered during his first days at Columbia. "Ginsberg and Burroughs came to the Nuyorican," he explains, but, at least initially, "the Nuyoricans did not go to those parties." They had their own world downtown, where, he says, "Miguel was the mayor of the block. There were more poets per square foot in that block than there were probably in the rest of the country. Jorge Brandon was literally on the street giving out his poetry. And I was lucky enough to run into him. He had a shopping cart full of his signed paintings and was wearing a construction helmet. . . . He was literally on the street hustling for his jobs as a sign painter and giving away his poems about Roberto Clemente and other Puerto Rican cultural touchstones. And in his shopping cart was his painting gear."

In his poem "Traffic Misdirector," Pedro Pietri captures some of the dynamic that Holman describes here:

the greatest living poet
in new york city
was born in Puerto Rico
his name is Jorge Brandon (1902–1995)
he is over 70 years old
he carries his metaphor
in brown shopping bags
inside steel shopping cart
he travels around with
on the streets of manhattan
he recites his poetry
to whoever listens
& when nobody is around
he recites to himself
he speaks the wisdom
of unforgettable palm trees
the vocabulary of coconuts
that wear overcoats
the traffic lights
of his poems function
without boring advice
from ac or dc current
book stores & libraries
are deprived of his vibes
to become familiar
with this immortal poet
you have to hang-out

on street corners
building stoops rooftops
fire escapes bars parks
subway train stations
bodegas botánicas
iglesias pawn shops
card games cock fights
funerals valencia bakery
hunts point palace
pool halls orchard beach
& cuchifrito stands
on the lower eastside
the admission is free
his presence is poetry.[15]

Holman and Pietri alike paint a vision of both a particular poetry scene and a cast of characters in full possession of their powers, lovely, luxurious, and unabashed, taking on the weight of their moment with real dignity and quite a bit of flair.

There were, in New York City, few more vocal supporters of the art of slam than Bob Holman. And though he was eventually replaced as host of the slam at the Nuyorican, he nonetheless continued to have an impact on the city's spoken word community for years to come, as a cofounder of the Mouth Almighty record label—which signed and promoted poets, in addition to having its own slam team that won NPS in 1997—and as the founder of the Bowery Poetry Club, which he started in 2002. The Bowery would eventually become, alongside Bar 13 and the Nuyo, one of the three major venues for spoken word in New York City through the first part of the twenty-first century.

In the generation after Holman, another poet who came to slam through the printed page was Willie Perdomo. Long before Perdomo stepped to a microphone to read poems, books, he says, were "like internal subway systems." With a book in his hand, he could go anywhere, be anything. And then came the epiphany that he one day wanted to compose books all his own. "The first instance that I had of aspiring to be a writer was after reading *Down These Mean Streets* by Piri Thomas. And that year was, I think was [my] freshman year in high school. It was a pivotal and impressionable year for me, because not only did I read Piri Thomas's *Down These Mean Streets,* but I also heard poetry read aloud for the first time by Ed Randolph, who is an African American poet. They called him the Mad Poet of Harlem, and he was a contemporary of Sekou Sundiata." Randolph was also a receptionist at Friends Seminary, which Perdomo attended during his middle- and high-school years. At an assembly one day, he read a few poems. "And this language that was in the poetry was similar to the language that I was hearing every day, but never had the idea that I could put that language on paper." This language, Perdomo tells me, was exceedingly rich in vernacular, and not just in terms of diction: it was also a "spiritual, cultural vernacular"—something that was true to his ear, his sense of himself in the world, in a way that the poetry he was reading in the classroom at that time simply wasn't. Listening to Ed Randolph helped him give himself permission to keep an "ear to the street, as it were" to take the language of the neighborhood and bring it to the page.

This approach would be a hallmark of Perdomo's writing for years to come. He published a book, *Where a Nickel Costs a Dime* in 1996, and, he says, "It was a wonderful thing for me to be in the old B. Dalton's on Sixth Avenue and Eighth Street across from the Gray's Papaya hot-dog stand and see a book that I had written in the P section of the poetry section next to Sylvia Plath and Edgar Allan Poe." He saw himself as a writer in print before he had read a poem aloud. But eventually, "I started seeing folks like Amiri Baraka read aloud. Sonia Sanchez read aloud. Pedro Pietri read aloud. Sandra Maria Esteves read aloud. So I have all these models of what poetry could actually sound like and how poets were able to lift the words off of their page." Perdomo goes on: "Because if you see any reading by Baraka, for the most part he reads off manuscript, and he just lifts those words off of the page as if the page was a score."

Perdomo had yet to discover the poetry slam scene for himself. It happened through Paul Beatty, whose poems, like Perdomo's, had appeared in the literary supplement of a black paper called *The City Sun*. (There was more than one black paper in the city back then, he reminds me.) The *Sun* had just published "Nigger-Reecan Blues" (a poem Perdomo would eventually recite on *Def Poetry* in 2004 to uproarious applause) in the early nineties, and around that time they met at an NYU reading put together by Kevin Powell, the author and cultural critic. "It was about fifty or so young African American and Latinx poets coming through . . . you had Janice Lowe coming through, Sharan Strange coming through. And then you had Asha Bandele, Tony Medina, Kevin Young. All these poets from all parts of the country, and Paul Beatty happened to be there." He and Beatty struck up a conversation, and Beatty told him "that there was this scene going on at the Nuyorican Poets Cafe." Perdomo says, "I had read about him in *The Village Voice*. I really didn't know what a slam was, but what really interested me was the mention of the Nuyorican, because by that point, I had already read an anthology on Nuyorican poetry, the original from the seventies that really set the blueprint for what it is to be a Nuyorican poet." (The anthology was Algarín's 1975 *Nuyorican Poetry*.) "So when I read the article in *The Village Voice*," Perdomo goes on, "I highlighted the phrase 'Nuyorican Poets Cafe.' And here was Paul Beatty himself saying, 'You should come down and come to the slam.'" Perdomo says, "I was, like, 'Cool.' So Friday night I come down, and this is the first time I meet Bob Holman. And Paul says, 'This is Willie.' Introducing me to Bob. 'He's going to read tonight.' The first poet gets up there, man . . . and they hold up scores for the poems."

Perdomo was shocked—so much so that he actually exclaimed aloud to Holman, "Yo, what is this?!" "You didn't know?" Holman replied, surprised that Perdomo was unaware of the intense level of competition he had just signed up for. Nevertheless, after "two forty-ounces of St. Ides or something like that," Perdomo went up onstage and "read the hell out those poems, man. I was so scared." And then it just kept happening. Perdomo kept reading, and kept winning, and kept returning to the Nuyorican for more. The highlight of those performances in the early nineties, he reminds me, was not the notoriety, really, but the sense that poem by poem, slam by slam, he was becoming a part of a tradition at the Nuyorican that preceded him. "It was like reading in front of your heroes," he tells me, and I can hear his voice illuminate as he lists their names: Bimbo Rivas, Pedro Pietri—the vanguard, the founders of the Nuyorican school in which he was now creating his own legend. This was where Perdomo learned how to be a working poet in the world. If nothing else, it meant being part of an endless ensemble. During his first months at the Nuyo, Bob asked him to join a traveling collective of poets he was putting together, a group that included Dael Orlandersmith, Tracie Morris, reg e. gaines, Mike Tyler, Ed Morales, and Edwin Torres. Perdomo emphasizes, importantly, that they "didn't all sound the same," which was central to Holman's vision. Before long, this newly assembled company hit the open road: they went international, traveled to Europe—"a nice run while it lasted," Perdomo recalls. But this was also an inevitable turning point for the local culture of the Nuyo. "That was really the moment when the Nuyorican went from being one of New York City's best-kept secrets," he says. "It was underground. There were no velvet ropes outside. There was no mural. There wasn't even a sign that said Nuyorican Poets Cafe. It was just a gray door with a dump behind it. And if you walked by it, you wouldn't know that you had just passed the Nuyorican Poets Cafe." He adds that around this period, "gentrification started to sort of dip its toe into the water. And so that scene that was underground had its own culture. It was very familiar. There was a family atmosphere to the scene."

As the venue grew more and more popular, however, this precious anonymity—what we might think of, following the poet Bob Kaufman, as being "involved with uninvolvement"—would eventually wear away.[16] Mainstream media outlets began featuring the Nuyorican, and the Cafe became a hotspot for travelers from around the world. "MTV comes through, PBS starts coming through, *New York* magazine starts coming through," Perdomo recalls, "and you can see that the scene is about to get commercialized. It's about to get commodified. For better or for worse." This early nineties era in spoken word Perdomo describes included unprecedented attention to spoken word on television: e.g., the *Fighting Wordz* commercial spots on MTV (which featured poets like Maggie Estep and reg e. gaines reading their original work) or *Spoken Word Unplugged* (a spoken word concert series that was also on television on MTV). In a 1994 *Variety* magazine article describing the *Free Your Mind* tour—which would serve as source material for *Spoken Word Unplugged*—Adam Sandler writes:

> Giving new meaning to the buzz phrase "free your mind," MTV will launch its first spoken-word tour, spotlighting the work of three top poets. The twenty-city *Free Your Mind* tour launches today and will hit college campuses and cities nationwide. It will include spoken-word artists reg e. gaines, Maggie Estep—whose style has been dubbed "rant 'n' roll" —and John S. Hall. The tour also will feature celeb appearances by recording artists such as Speech from Arrested Development and Evan Dando of the Lemonheads. MTV will sponsor contests at each stop, giving local poets the opportunity to win an opening spot on the show's bill.[17]

A later example of this phenomenon would be *The United States of Poetry,* a five-part PBS series that Bob Holman hosted in 1996, still six years before *Def Poetry Jam* would arrive on the scene.

Clearly, this sort of media attention and corporate investment represented a major shift from the sense of general anonymity Perdomo attributes to the spoken word scene of only a few years prior. Importantly, he sees two sides to this moment in which poetry slam begins to gain global popularity. It was both the loss of something precious and a tremendous victory. "Because were it not for this scene, you wouldn't have thousands—I mean millions—of kids writing poems right now. Because that's really what it was. It was a springboard into an international culture that just was blazing. And you would go to these cities, do workshops, read in major performance venues and be at the BBC one day and the Sorbonne the next. It was exciting to be a young poet during that time, learning how to read poems aloud. Because it's not just about the performance. What most folks don't understand about spoken word is that you learn how to edit your poems on the spot."

Whether your poem was already well polished or fresh off the page, inchoate, barely legible between the cross-outs and new additions to the opening stanza, there was a place for it in the Nuyorican scene. The world of the Nuyo and the prominence of slam there as the 2000s rolled around allowed for what Tyehimba Jess described to me as "building community through an open mic." As he put it, "You build a certain level of literacy through the open mic. It's a great place to start. A probing, questioning mind that's deeply interested in the form will take that as a starting point and go forward from there. As far as I'm concerned, the slam is just a rigorous, competitive open mic."

Jive Poetic, who hosted my own first slam at the Nuyorican, was drawn in by that competitive spirit. He didn't discover the art of spoken word until his college years, when he arrived on the campus of SUNY Buffalo. He competed in his first Wednesday-night slam at the Nuyorican in 2001. He was immediately hooked. More than anything else, it was the tactical element of the slam that drew him in. He realized that there were actual strategies, teams with historic runs, an energy you could feel in the atmosphere comparable to that of the competitive sports arenas he had grown up in. What he also loved was that the Nuyorican wasn't the only venue with this kind of environment at the time: the Bowery and Bar 13 were other poetry venues within walking distance of

2003 NUYORICAN NATIONAL SLAM TEAM

From Left to Right: Jive Poetic; Julian Curry, 2003 Grand Slam Champion; Karen Jaime, Nuyorican Slam Hostess; Anacoana, Team Alternate; Felice Belle, Team Coach; Kenaya & Carlos Gomez. Photo by Clare Ultimo.

each other and the Nuyo, all in lower Manhattan, quietly revolutionizing the spoken word landscape. You could move between venues, between slams and teams and open mic scenes, trying out different material in front of different audiences to see what worked, and for what type of crowd. For Jive, this made every return to the Nuyorican feel special—so much so that in 2003 he joined the Nuyorican team, alongside Julian Curry, Hostage, and Carlos Andrés Gomez, whose work I would discover two years later via Myspace.

After Jive made the Nuyorican team, he came back a few times throughout the slam season. But he remembers one evening in particular, when he realized that he might need to spend less time on the road and more cultivating the relationships at the Cafe that were meaningful to him. "I came back one night to perform at an open mic. After I got offstage, one of the poets in the audience stopped me and said, 'Man, I can't wait till you start slamming.' And I thought to myself, 'This is crazy—I'm in my city and they don't recognize me.'" That realization inspired Jive to change his approach: "And then it dawned on me. What am I really contributing to the environment that nurtured me to do this thing?" From that point on, Jive decided to come around a bit more. In 2006, Mahogany L. Browne, poet, young-adult fiction author, and nationally renowned slam coach, became the Wednesday-night host, and eventually the host of Friday nights at the Nuyo. Jive then moved into the Wednesday slot as the host of the slam.

For many, the Nuyo stage afforded an opportunity for personal reinvention. Consider the late hip-hop legend Daniel Dumile, widely known by the moniker MF DOOM (inspired by the Marvel Comics villain, Doctor Doom). Born in London in 1971, Dumile moved with his family to Long Island as a child. In the mid-1980s he would emerge into the underground American hip-hop scene under the pseudonym Zev Love X as part of a group he started with his younger brother, DJ Subroc, and a friend of theirs, Jade 1 (who would eventually leave the group, and be replaced by Onyx the Birthstone Kid). They called themselves KMD, an acronym for Kausing Much Damage. Dumile's first appearance on record was as a guest on 3rd Bass's 1989 hit "The Gas Face," a term he claimed to have invented.* It would be two more years before KMD completed their debut album, *Mr. Hood*. Two years after that, in 1993, Subroc was tragically killed by a motorist, while attempting to cross the Long Island Expressway.

In the wake of his brother's death, Dumile all but disappeared from the scene. KMD's record label, Elektra, refused to shelve their follow-up album, and he decided to disassemble what remained of the group. The twentysomething MC instead chose to focus on family—spending much of this time away from the stage raising his son—in addition to preparing for the next phase of his journey as an artist. This four-year period, 1994 to 1998, was a time of total transformation for Dumile. He bought new recording equipment, moved back and forth between New York and Atlanta, and created a range of alter egos, several of which would later reappear on records as variations on a central theme: villainy.

---

* In Dumile's own words: "I came up with the term 'gas face'—it's just that face you make when you shocked or surprised. Like when somebody catches you off guard."

Then, seemingly emerging ex nihilo from the darkness, Dumile appeared, fully formed on the stage of the Nuyorican, wearing a red Phillies cap, a stocking mask, and a new name: Metal Face Doom.

Or, as most of us now know him, MF DOOM. When asked by *Wire* magazine about the new persona, Dumile had this to say: "It don't matter what we look like, it's just the sound of the music. The mask is the stiffest face—it don't change none, it just got that mean kind of look to it. So you want to look at something? Look at that. It don't matter what I look like, what chain I got on, how I'm dressed, nothing—it's just the microphone and the spitfire." In other venues, he would say that the mask was an homage to *The Phantom of the Opera*, that the recording industry had deformed him, required him to shield us from his visage. The new, metallic mask DOOM is referencing—he would eventually swap out the stocking cap he donned at the Nuyo—was made for him by the artist Blake Lethem, aka KEO, who based the new model on one of the helmets worn by Russell Crowe in the 2000 film *Gladiator*.

This was the version of DOOM that I encountered as a college freshman in 2006, two years after he released *MM . . . FOOD*—an anagram of MF DOOM—which I listened to repeatedly in those days, navigating the poetry scene of West Philadelphia, fascinated by the fact of this mysterious man with a persona pulled from the very comics that shaped so much of my imaginative landscape in childhood. In pulling from the world-destroying mythos of Victor Von Doom—archnemesis of the Fantastic Four and one of the major villains in the Marvel universe—DOOM dared to embrace a narrative of not only lawlessness, but invention and unrepentant genius, that I found compelling. This combined with the fact that he was rhyming in patterns that were layered to the point of a kind of luxury feel ("Tired of the wait / till the villain bring deliverance from the dire straits / fire at a higher rate / while they make the liars fliers scatter / buy a plate /

isolate the wires"). Or else truly anthemic, if still somewhat self-effacing, in their sense of affirmation ("he wears a mask just to cover the raw flesh / a rather ugly brother with flows that's gorgeous"). DOOM's music became a soundtrack to that era of my young adulthood, as I traveled back and forth between Philly and New York, and eventually out into the world as a full-time arts educator and performance artist.

March Forth

My Nuyorican experience changed the course of my life. I won that first slam with my poem "Talented Tenth," and three weeks later I made the 2006 New York team that reached the semifinals of the Brave New Voices International Youth Poetry Slam, which was also held in NYC that year. The following summer, I would join the 2007 Philadelphia team that won the entire competition. It was the beginning of a journey that I never could have imagined in advance.

I knew from both clips on Myspace and word of mouth that the University of Pennsylvania had some incredible poets—Carlos Andrés Gómez and Caroline Rothstein were my introduction to the world of collegiate spoken word—and I met one of them, Ben Alisuag, at Brave New Voices that year. Ben and I would share a stage at the NAACP Image Awards three years later, but when we first met, he was just an eighteen-year-old representing the Philadelphia team on the finals stage, and I was a high-school senior in the audience, floored by the passion and unchecked imagination of the performances I saw onstage that night. After finals were over, I approached Ben and told him that I would be attending

Penn the following year. He offered me his congratulations and invited me to audition for the Excelano Project, Penn's premier spoken word collective.

Alongside its academic reputation and relative proximity to New York (close enough that I could visit my parents on weekends, but far enough that neither would easily drop by unannounced), the reasons I chose Penn for undergrad were the social life—the best house party I had ever been to was during the admitted students' weekend—and the spoken word scene. Weeks before I submitted my application, I listened to the poems of two EP members in particular—"What's Genocide" and "41" from Carlos Andrés Gomez, and "They Call Me Granola" and "Noah" from Caroline Rothstein—more times than I could count on those days when I was still trying to find my voice as a teenage poet competing in youth slams around the city, preparing for the Brave New Voices competition that summer. I remember being struck even then, first and foremost, by the aesthetic differences between the poets—content, cadence, speed of delivery—as well as the undeniable passion that they had in common.

I spent the rest of the summer practicing. I wrote new poems in my Mead spiral notebook. And I remembered the conversation that I had with Ben, who was fresh off a CUPSI run where Penn lost in the finals to the University of New Mexico. In his first full year of slam competition, he was two for two on finals appearances and thus, it seemed to me at seventeen, might be a useful resource for someone new to the form.

Ben grew up in the Bay Area, in Hayward. One of his teachers at Tennyson High School brought him to a Youth

Speaks event when he was in tenth grade. He made his initial attempt at writing a poem shortly thereafter. The first spoken word poem was about his relationship with his father, which would become a central theme of his writing. Later that academic year, one of his classmates organized a poetry slam at Tennyson, and Ben signed up. It was the first time he had ever read his work in public. After that, he went to the Youth Speaks competition in San Francisco every year. During his first few days at Penn, he attended the performing arts showcase, which featured representatives from various groups at Penn, and saw Caroline Rothstein perform. It lit a fire under him. For the first time since that Youth Speaks event, he started writing again. Ben decided that he would audition for Excelano a week later, even though it required that he not only compose but *memorize* two poems to present to the group. He got in on his first try.

Excelano's origin story is a compelling one, and is told best, perhaps, by Carlos Andrés Gómez. Over the years, he has become an award-winning writer and performer in multiple genres: spoken word, the printed page (his debut collection, *Fractures,* was the winner of the Felix Pollak Prize in Poetry in 2020), and the silver screen (he appeared in Spike Lee's *Inside Man*). Gómez grew up in Providence, Rhode Island, and was seventeen when he first saw the movie *Slam*. According to him, the film changed the trajectory of his life—he watched it three times and then, at two a.m., he tells me, "I just picked up a pen and I found some scrap paper and I wrote until nine in the morning."

The year was 1999. In the process of discovering his own, unique voice—which included learning more about the poetry slam practitioners who'd inspired him—Carlos, still just a senior in high school, visited his father in New York, and decided to make a pilgrimage to the Nuyo. He describes the events of that evening as a radiant blur. He was hooked immediately. Once he got back home to Providence, Carlos started attending an open mic on Hope Street, at a venue called the Gallery Cafe. He went weekly and brought new work each time, sharing with a roomful of students from the neighboring colleges and universities—Brown University, Providence College, Rhode Island College—as well as a few other high school students, in what turned out to be his training ground for the Excelano Project.

Having honed his craft now for months in Providence's open mic scene, he decided it was time to make the move into poetry slam. Upon arriving at Penn, his journey began at an Old City venue called the Painted Bride, which held a slam on the first Friday of the month. The audience for First Friday was anywhere from 250 to 300 people. The slam had only one round. As many as 40 participants would compete—yes, you're reading that number correctly—and the winner would receive one hundred dollars in cash. The slam was hosted by Kevin O'Neil, and not unlike the Nuyorican in its prime was frequented by artists from across the worlds of hip-hop and R&B: Black Thought, Bahamadia, Jill Scott. There was an intensity in that room, Carlos tells me, that's hard to explain. But he eventually found his way. He slammed every single month during his freshman year before the season culminated in a Grand Slam at the end of spring. When the dust settled, Carlos, at the age of eighteen, was named Grand Slam Champion of the Painted Bride. And though the win itself was a personal milestone, what he describes much more vividly than the competition itself is what it taught him about the slam format and its relationship to audience attention. He had never seen a poetry audience focus as intently as they did when they were watching a slam—"People never listened that carefully in an open mic," he tells me—and it wasn't just about the structure of the competition. The slam, as far as he could tell, was evoking something new in him, and in the other poets he knew from the scene. He saw writers he'd watched multiple times in other environments become someone barely recognizable, unlocking another level of intensity, and presence, they had barely hinted at before. This fascinated Carlos. What was it about the pressure of the slam that initiated this effect? And was it a good thing?

That fall, Carlos would meet Mahogany L. Browne and Jive Poetic, make the Nuyorican team, and cement his place in that particular tradition, all while he was still a freshman in college. Back at Penn, his love for the craft of the spoken word was taking on a different form. Through the Center for Community Partnerships, he taught a creative writing class at Edison/Fareira High School alongside his Penn classmates Jess Brand and Warren Longmire, who proctored other courses. Warren taught coding back then, but eventually admitted to Carlos that he was also a poet.

Carlos, now a seasoned stage performer in his own right, figured that the Painted Bride might be a perfect venue for his newfound friend to try out his work in front of other people, and hone what was clearly an original voice. Warren agreed, and the pair headed to the Painted Bride and continued to sharpen their work there, in a community of Philadelphia writers and musicians. "I wish we had something like this at Penn," they thought—and so they made it happen. Warren and another friend, Joy Dyer, eventually applied to the Performing Arts Council at Penn to have their idea for the Excelano Project, a spoken word performance collective, receive university funding. "They rejected us unanimously," Carlos recalls. "We didn't get one vote."

Carlos's dream of creating a group that reflected the spoken word world he already knew well—one filled with writers who were black, brown, queer, poor, neurodivergent, and systemically disenfranchised, students who had historically been excluded from Penn as an institution, or else marginalized within its borders—faced a level of narrow-mindedness he all but expected. The first Performing Arts Council vote made clear that such stories, such unruly presence, was not welcome at that time within the performing arts community at Penn. Having spent considerable time now on the open mic scene in Providence, at the Nuyorican, and at the Painted Bride, where hundreds of people would flock to hear the news of the day recited in verse that shook the room, Carlos knew the true power of the genre. "As a son of a Colombian immigrant, as a person who didn't learn to read until he was nine years old, as somebody who constantly felt like I was on the outside," bringing this particular kind of group to the University of Pennsylvania, an Ivy League campus in the middle of West Philadelphia, was especially important to him. It was meant to be the ground of a certain kind of disruption, a shout in the darkness you couldn't ignore. Even after this initial rejection, and without official recognition from the university, the group continued to grow. Due to PAC policy, the group couldn't appeal until the fall of Carlos's sophomore year. The second time around, the young poet decided to take matters into his own hands. He delivered a speech in front of the committee:

> I'm not going to justify the way this group obviously fits the rubric of what's required to have an organization welcome to the Performing Arts Council because there's no one else that is doing performance poetry or spoken word at this university. I'm going to look all of you in the eye. I know every single one of you unanimously rejected this. But I also know that you don't want to be a part of that legacy. I believe that every single one of you are going to see and recognize the power and the importance of this group and the impact that it will have on this campus. That every single one of you are going to change your vote. And that, on appeal, you're going to accept this group.

This time around, the Excelano Project received a unanimous vote in their favor. Carlos later got word that Excelano was the first performing-arts group in Penn's history to be admitted successfully on appeal: a fitting start for a collective that would go on to be exceedingly controversial, especially for its outspoken opposition to the war in Iraq, its unrelenting critique of Penn's gentrification of West Philadelphia and its displacement of residents of the Black Bottom, as well as for its engagement with a host of other societal issues. All this while the poets continued to make a name for themselves through packed performances across campus and success at

CUPSI, the national collegiate slam. But what must also be remembered, Carlos reminds me, is the sense of camaraderie, even family, that the Excelano Project has been able to cultivate over the years. I experienced this myself: from my first show as a freshman to my final showcase senior year, Carlos and several Excelano alumni were always present. They reminded us to keep our eyes open, to *get free*. What undergirded this commitment of time and energy for Carlos, and what was passed down to me, Ben, and our peers, was a sense of his own relationship to spoken word as one marked by an *insistence on his own survival*. Poems were a way to speak back to a social order that cared little about who he was or the truths he knew bone-deep, the communities he felt allegiance to, the love that kept him going.

Carlos helped to inspire many other poets to take up the Excelano mantle during their time at Penn. One of the first was Caroline Rothstein. Caroline was a triple-threat performer from childhood: a singer, actor, and dancer pursuing those arts in a suburb outside of Chicago while dreaming of life as a working artist in the big city. Her plan was to star in a hit play on Broadway—"be the next Bette Midler" is how she describes it—and also write works of nonfiction. She composed a fair amount of poetry growing up, but as a performer she identified primarily as a student and practitioner of musical theater. This love for the stage would come to be a major influence not only on her approach to the art form we share, but on her work as an activist, which is in some ways inextricable from it.

In 2002, during the spring of the gap year she took after high school, Caroline was admitted to Penn. While visiting the campus for Penn Previews, a long-standing university program where admitted students visit campus, Caroline discovered spoken word. "It was Spring Fling weekend, and this guy Carlos is onstage with a bunch of other people and they're doing this poem. I've never seen people do poems the way they're doing poems. The refrain is 'They call me anti-American / because I'm pro-humanitarian.'" Caroline, who as a child had been taken to see Mark Kitchell's documentary *Berkeley in the Sixties* by her father and believed that one of the major benefits of living on a college campus was the chance to further deepen one's relationship to protest—and, what's more, that patriotism *meant* protest ("That's what I thought America was," she says)—realized that she "wanted to find people that I could get angry about America with."

At long last, she had found them, a group committed not only to a kind of righteous anger about the American status quo at the turn of the century, but also to a real joy, humor, and tenderness that would pervade the work they created as a group.

Now here's where things went off the rails. Caroline's housing form got lost in the mail. She was slotted into the high-rises—which were not her first choice among the dorms at Penn—with two roommates from the Bay Area, both of whom were committed to radical visions of political change, which made Caroline feel right at home. They were the only freshmen on the entire floor. One of her neighbors, she soon discovered, was an engineering student from North Philadelphia named Warren Longmire. Three floors above her, she would also discover, was Obi Obisanya, another member of the Excelano Project. At that point, she was introduced to

Carlos, and decided to try out for Excelano at the end of her freshman fall.

Caroline's original plan had been to maintain her arts practices from high school: musical theater, a cappella, all of it. She even got callbacks for several of the performing-arts groups she had auditioned for in the weeks prior. But the genres she had loved and spent most of her life studying felt like they no longer fit her present needs. She would require a new set of materials to tell this next part of her story. All her forms, she realized, would soon fuse into one. "I spent my life being other characters," Caroline tells me. "Now, I needed to be myself."

Caroline joined the Excelano Project, and the transformation was immediate: "Because I could now embody my truth while saying it out loud, instead of just writing it on a page to live on a page, or instead of performing it as someone else. I was having to give voice and embodiment to my story and my politics in a way that saved my life." She used every instrument available to hone her inner voice and grow more skilled as a writer and performer. She signed up for a new course, English 88, which was a survey on modern and contemporary poetry that took place at Penn's Kelly Writers House. She memorized Maggie Estep's "Sex Goddess of the Western Hemisphere." And in 2004, she competed in her first-ever poetry slam, which was a qualifying slam for Penn's CUPSI team. It was her first win.

That year's CUPSI competition would bring Caroline and the other Penn poets to the campus of UC Berkeley, where they were slated to compete against more than fifty other teams from across the country. There, Caroline had an epiphany. There were a number of poets at the competition whose entire understanding of what spoken word was, what it could accomplish, was routed through the slam. Rather than standing apart as an especially vivid, public, popular arm of the larger genre of the spoken word, poetry slam was assumed to be everything—an end unto itself. For Caroline, slam was simply an excuse to get out and perform for an audience. It was "the default that got [her] to do more poems." This stance emerged, she recognizes, from the unique training she received from the Excelano Project not only as a stand-alone collective, but as part of a unique arts ecosystem at Penn, which provided funds and facilities to many performance arts groups across campus throughout the year. As an organization under the aegis of Penn's Performing Arts Council, Excelano was guaranteed resources to do a full-scale production each year. This, as you might imagine, was a real rarity among the college and university slam teams that attended CUPSI that year, and well into the future. That level of support, at the very least, meant that for a number of Excelano poets throughout the years, it wasn't just that slam wasn't their only or primary way into the form, it was that they had an entirely different trajectory: speech and debate, YouTube clips, theater—the list is extensive and expanding even still. Caroline's CUPSI experience was the first of many where she came to understand slam, if not as an entryway into spoken word as such, then as an instrument through which a more rigorous approach to the form might be developed. Slam was where you trained. It was where you tested your work in the forge of competition.

Caroline often took the leadoff, or A slot, in a slam. These are the poets who, on a team, would go up first and take the temperature of a room, unlike poets in the C slot (the penultimate performance) or the anchor/D slot—the poet/poets/poem who brings it all home. This was something we shared: the experience of performing in that opening slot, which felt like a mutual act of trust; the team gives you the responsibility of being the first voice the crowd hears, and in return they back you up, no matter how it goes.

Various films and televised documentaries chronicled this period of slam's heyday and the flowering of young poets finding spaces in which their craft, their voices, could be strengthened in community. The youth-centered literary arts organization Youth Speaks, which helped shape Ben's path in high school, was founded in 1996. From the very beginning, poetry slam was one of its core programs. It hosted its first poetry slam in April 1997 in San Francisco—an interesting mirror of the first National Poetry Slam in the same city almost a decade earlier. A year later, in collaboration with the Connecticut-based poet and arts educator Elizabeth Thomas, Youth Speaks would cohost the first national youth slam, though it was not yet officially called the Brave New Voices competition. That first national slam featured five teams. The second would be held in Albuquerque, New Mexico, in 1999, and featured the same teams, which hailed from San Francisco, New York City, the Navajo Nation, Ann Arbor, and Connecticut. This slam was the subject of PBS's *Poetic License*, the second spoken-word documentary of its kind, only a few years after *SlamNation* and *Slam* set the tone for spoken word on film.

The documentary begins with an epigraph drawn from

Audre Lorde's "The Transformation of Silence into Language and Action": "What are the words you do not yet have? What do you need to say?"[18] This is followed by a mélange of youth poets reciting verses before the first two adults we hear converse in plain speech: Bob Holman and James Kass, who will return throughout the film in a recurring role as cultural insiders, translators to the documentary audience. They are joined in this effort by an all-star cast of poets, educators, and organizers: Marc Bamuthi Joseph, Sekou Sundiata, Asha Bandele, and Abiodun Oyewole from the Last Poets. Seeing Abiodun's face in particular brings me back in time, as I remember the parties he threw in his living room in the early 2000s, when I was still in college, back in uptown NYC for the summer. Everyone there, it seemed, was a poet or a musician. In *Poetic License*, Abiodun appears in a similar role, as a mentor and teacher, coaching one of the New York City youth poets.

There is barely any sense of the actual competition in the first seventeen minutes or so of the film. Most of what we see are shots of individual performances from a mosaic of young people, most of them named though others are not, and you can't exactly tell whether they are performing at an open mic or a slam—there is no explicit mention of the scores, for instance—though we are led to assume the latter. The competition begins around 17:57 with the New York City team, and a slam at the Apollo Theater featuring seventeen-year-old Asheena Campbell, who reminds me of the poets I grew up alongside, as she talks about writing poems on the train. The NYC team, we soon find, will not be able to make it to the first-ever national youth slam, because there are no adults to take them. The moment is addressed only in the form of a brief line of white text onscreen, but resonates throughout the rest of the film. One is reminded, in that moment, that these are all young people, competing for the first time in a form made for adults, and *necessarily relying on adults to do so.*[*] For this reason, the film's eventual plot twist is all the more surprising, and in the best possible way.

After an opening night that features performances that are, fittingly, as diverse and unfettered and clearly in-process as the teenage poets themselves (many are reciting with their eyes closed, off of notepads, offering introductions before their poems), we are fast-forwarded through the clips of the competition until we reach the finals stage. The first half of the slam proceeds as planned. But at intermission, there's a tectonic shift: the poets have decided to cancel the competition, to go on strike (it's important to mention here that this is the exact language they use to describe their refusal of slam convention), and throw a party. The film ends with a stunning solo performance from one of the Bay Area poets and a montage of the young writers talking about their experiences, not of slam as such, but with spoken word as a form, and in the literary communities they have come to know and cherish.

Poetic License would not be the last time that the world of youth poetry slam was captured on film. In 2009, *HBO Presents: Brave New Voices* arrived: a multipart television series that followed several teams—from New York, Phila-

---

[*] Another such reminder appears midway through the film, when Marc Smith appears in the crowd, unexpectedly and without being identified by the film's narrator (which feels like the "So what!" ethos turned up to ten).

delphia, Honolulu, Ft. Lauderdale, and Ann Arbor—as they
prepared for the 2008 Brave New Voices festival in Wash-
ington DC. HBO filmed each team in its local rehearsal
spaces before heading to DC to document the progress of
these teams throughout the competition. To James Kass and
his colleagues at Youth Speaks, the series would only further
the core goal toward which they were always working: to
create public arenas where youth voices could be heard. In
exchange, according to Susan Weinstein's book on the youth
spoken-word poetry movement, *The Room Is on Fire,* "HBO
offered a small sponsorship of Brave New Voices, and paid
a licensing fee to have the exclusive rights to film the 2008
festival, as well as to use the name 'Brave New Voices.'"[19] Yet,
for some of the coaches and youth poets, the constant pres-
ence of TV cameras was seen as a distraction and, for some,
changed the experience of the festival from one of communal
camaraderie to one that was irreversibly commodified. Our
Philadelphia team that year, for example, ended up forfeiting
on finals stage and opting to use that opportunity to recite
the four poems, all group pieces, that meant the most to us.
We realized that we had gotten entirely too caught up in the
competitive element of the festival—this after successfully
challenging our loss in the semifinal round on the basis of a
time penalty, which is a rare sight at the youth level given the
spirit of the proceedings. During our team meeting before
the bout, the five of us took a vote and decided that we had
to make a different choice while we still had the chance. At
its core, after all, the festival was supposed to be a way to feel
a little bit less alone; to share new work and meet people you
never would have otherwise. It was about building space to

gather, on one accord, and celebrate the art that enlivened our days.

For Jive Poetic, the joy of coaching and mentoring young people from New York City on their journey through BNV (or hosting at slams where they perform, as he did for me), was seeing the sense of unity and accomplishment they get to experience when they meet young people in love with the art from other cities and towns across the world—seeing the ways of working through the most pressing social and political issues of the day that are otherwise barred from the sphere of our attention or obligation. The witness of youth poets is an unrelenting critique and anchoring presence. It reminds us what it is, exactly, that makes this work worth doing, how we might, to borrow a phrase from Toni Morrison, "do the work of a world worthy of life."[20]

Jive tells me the story of one of his teammates, Hostage, with whom he made it to the NPS finals during their 2003 run with the Nuyorican team, and this particular teammate, he recounts, retired from poetry slam immediately after this last leg of the competition. "He retired right there. And I thought, 'This doesn't make any kind of sense. You've only been doing this for a couple of years. You talking about retiring.' He said, 'I'm out. This is it.' At the time he did get some college gigs, and that was it. And he didn't slam again." Jive reflects on the deeper meaning of competition in the realm of spoken word, saying, "Some people are going to have careers in this. They're going to be on TV. They're going to be recording artists. They're going to have book deals. And some people are not. That's just the statistics. So what if we created a new space that embodies this momentum but is a whole different form? It's got to grow. It's got to evolve into something else. Young people going to look at it and say it's antiquated and be like, 'What's this? This is all we doing?'"

Before the most recent National Poetry Slam competition, Jive gave the Brooklyn team he was coaching a choice: "We can go to this Nationals, together, which might be the last one ever, or we can create an original showcase in Antigua for the people out there." The Brooklyn team chose the latter, clarifying for Jive that going to Nationals wasn't their best shot at "going pro," anyway. They had the Internet now. The national stage was all around these poets, every day. Which also meant that they could put on the showcase and get the work directly to the people without the added stress of competition. What is the role of slam, of a physical venue or scene, in a world like that?

Book 3:

THE DIGITAL REVOLUTION IN SPOKEN WORD

Our real difficulty arises from the fact that, unlike the oral poet, we are not accustomed to thinking in terms of fluidity. We find it difficult to grasp something that is multiform. It seems to us necessary to construct an ideal text or to seek an original, and we remain dissatisfied with an ever-changing phenomenon. I believe that once we know the facts of oral composition we must cease trying to find an original of any traditional song. From one point of view each performance is an original.

—Albert Lord

Education is the relation between diverse generations, and contact is its mode of transmission. For example, an artist is capable of affecting, in and of themselves, a line of transmission from Paleolithic art through to contemporary art, and this transmission is a relationship to time, to human—I don't like the word "human," so perhaps we could say "mortal"— experience. These lines are within the artist, not made manifest by him or her, nor are they structures of representation, and they are put into effect through their practice, through the contact with them.

—Bernard Stiegler

When performed by the author, it can feel almost cathartic to those watching: we carry our own feelings into the venue, and they are washed away and replaced by the feelings of those declaiming on stage. Our grief and love and life become suddenly more vivid, more worthy of attention . . . for a moment we become what we are reading, even if we have never felt those emotions before. And after all, what better way to read poetry than by listening to it?

—Carina Pereira

We came up with the name for our soon-to-be poetry super-group via Google Chat. The Atlantic Ocean and a five-hour time difference did little to slow us down as we cast fresh ideas for our new venture across the darkness. The form fit the occasion perfectly. Toya and I decided to call the collective The Strivers Row. Our inspiration for the moniker came from a distinguished enclave in the subterranean utopia commonly known as Harlem World, New York (to the more formal or else uninitiated, the neighborhood was also called the St. Nicholas Historic District). As early as the 1920s, this particular pair of blocks on 138th and 139th Streets was already well-known for both the unique elegance of its brownstones and the growing number of black professionals—mostly doctors, lawyers, and others working in varied administrative fields—who eventually came to call these buildings home. My sister and I grew up not too far from the neighborhood. Though our childhood stomping grounds were in the Bronx and Yonkers, respectively, our grandmother at various points owned and operated three beauty salons between Spanish Harlem and 125th Street. The most prominent of which was located right up the block from the famed Lenox Avenue soul food restaurant, Sylvia's, whose owner, and namesake, was a close friend of Grandma's.

When I began spending summer afternoons at the 125th Street shop, I was seven years old. I did not yet know how to spell the word "cosmetologist," but I loved that it reminded me of both comic books and comets, my favorite things back then. The older women in the salon would pay me a dollar whenever I spelled a word three syllables or longer: "malfeasance," "indubitable," "recalcitrant," "loquacious." When I went on an especially good run, I could walk into the neighborhood bodega with eight dollars of cold hard cash, stuffed as if contraband into my freshly ironed khaki shorts. Do you know how many Peanut Chews and Swedish Fish you can buy with eight dollars? A lot. To borrow a phrase from June Jordan: "I was a millionaire in love."

This was where I fell in love with language. I learned to maneuver it, to appreciate its strength. I came to adore the salon for the robust social life it held within its four blue walls. Yes, I was small, and still wore high socks. I had a high voice and a high-top fade, a laugh too big for my body. Yes, I was a black child in a country that despised us, and reminded us of that ire quite often, most frequently in the bodies of security guards at our school, or bus drivers who called the police on us when we acted up, or the prisons holding our cousins, parents, big brothers. There was no such thing as death in the salon, though. There was only the latest gossip and Motown-era Marvin Gaye on the radio, an entire atmosphere of sounds and smells too perfect to have been engineered on planet Earth. You could have filled a hundred beauty shops with what I didn't know back then. But I was acutely aware of a certain truth I have not forgotten since those days: what we built in that space was indeed a refuge, but it was also something infinitely greater than that. It was a world on and in our own terms. A haven and a home.

Within the bounds of this unaccredited arts academy

uptown, my sister and I became what my tenth-grade English teacher Ms. Simms would have called "semiprofessional elocutionists." We built playgrounds out of language in the salon, during the raucous car ride home, and in the living room after school while our parents were at work: freestyling rhyming stories, putting on entire stage productions with only pajamas and our grandmother's wigs for costumes. There was always poetry all around us. And in the occasional silences, we crafted our own. Over the years, I would learn that when I was a toddler, Toya translated my two-year-old glossolalia for the adults in the room, clarifying my cries, and otherwise making plain the incomprehensible on my behalf. As I grew, from baby boy to young poet and beyond, she remained there, stalwart and unfailingly creative, collaborating with me to create something unprecedented from the dreams only we could see.

2.

This was the history held within the name The Strivers Row. There was also, fittingly, now a double-entendre twist thrown in there via a fitting nautical metaphor: the idea of pressing forward through rough waters to get to whatever is next on the journey. Inspired as well, no doubt, by the fact of so many hundreds of miles of water between my sister and me as we continued to work through this new and altogether exciting idea. A bit of context that might be useful: during the era in question, the fall of 2011, I was living in Coventry, UK, studying for my MA in Theatre and Performance Studies at the University of Warwick, where I was a Marshall Scholar.

For those who might be unfamiliar (as I was only a few

months before I applied), the Marshall Scholarship dates back to 1953. It was created by the British Parliament as a "living gift" to the United States in recognition of Secretary of State George Marshall and the Marshall Plan. Up to fifty of these scholarships have been awarded every single year since 1954 by the Marshall Aid Commemoration Commission. They are given to college seniors and recent graduates across the United States to support graduate study at any UK institution. I was already applying to graduate school, and had planned to begin a research project that would combine my nascent interest in the intersection of African diaspora studies, disability studies, and performance theory. My search for the sorts of institutions that might support this work took some time, as well as more than a little bit of reaching out to former winners of the scholarship via email for insight. By the end of that part of the process, the University of Warwick was a clear choice. They had a top-ranked performance studies program, helmed by a fantastic group of faculty in my proposed area of focus. The campus wasn't too far from London, Oxford, or Cambridge via rail (just about every other Marshall Scholar in my cohort lived and studied in one of these three cities during my time there), but not so close that I could make the trip every other week. I would have no choice but to invest in my surroundings, make new friends, and focus on the project that inspired my transatlantic journey in the first place.

Looking back on the experience now, those first few months living in the UK were a clear influence on what would eventually become The Strivers Row. There was no formal coursework in my new program. The direction of my research, how much time I devoted each day to reading, writing, and editing, was totally up to me. I was the only Marshall Scholar in my cohort who had opted to attend Warwick, which forced me to spend most of those first weeks exploring the city and surrounding towns on my own. I was at all times left to my own devices: figuring out the bus routes and walking paths through trial and error, stumbling into places with names like Leamington Spa without a familiar voice from home to map the diverging pathways ahead.

In those earliest days abroad, I lived inside a strange and altogether unfamiliar, unexplored, loneliness. That is, until Faith, a new friend I had met on Twitter, intervened. Faith thought I should meet one of her friends, Sarah, who was also a student at the University of Warwick. In the weeks following our auspicious trip to the local buffet that Sarah invited me to, during one of my many solo trips into the city, I came across a local sneaker shop, Kong. This was in the city of Coventry proper, miles away from the Warwick campus, which had a much more rural feel to it. At Kong, I met a group of young men who would become some of my closest friends in the world: Kyle, Sam, Damola, and Julian. What I remember most clearly about that moment was meeting Kyle, who worked at Kong full-time. He was an expat from Chicago living and working in Coventry, and making lush, trippy dubstep and hip-hop instrumentals whenever he had the time. I became privy to both of these pieces of information rather unexpectedly, simply by asking whether the shop had a size 12 in a certain pair of black-and-yellow Nike SB Dunks in the back. Kyle heard my *American accent*, which was a phrase I had never encountered, and the look on his face changed almost immediately. We became fast friends.

Whenever I wasn't taking out new performance studies texts from the library (teaching yourself a new field from scratch is a tall order), or working on my MA thesis in my dorm room, I was at Kong listening to music, waiting for exclusive new drops, and picking up the national slang ("trainers," "mandem," "oh my days"). During those first few weeks hanging out with Kyle at the store, I eventually met the rest of the crew—Sam, Damola, and Julian—all of whom were students at nearby Coventry University.

At the time, Sam was also a member of a group called A Yellow Man (they would eventually go under the name Hawk House and put out a slew of beautiful records before retiring around 2015): an incredibly talented hip-hop and R&B trio out of South London that included a singer named Demae and Sam's little brother, Emmanuel. Damola was the comedian of our group. Julian was a poet and visual artist who shared my penchant for newsboy hats and well-crafted rap albums. Years after I left England, he remained, and remains, one of my closest friends. A few times a week, we all met up at Kong and listened to the latest radio hits and pored over oldies, finding common ground in the fact that even across our various homes in the diaspora—Nigeria, Sierra Leone, the United States—we had managed to discover a unifying language through the music we loved since we were children, every artist on the store playlist legendary enough that they only needed one name to identify them: Fela, Nina, Bob, Nas, Biggie, Lauryn, Sade.

In their own way, the familiar opening bars and bridges of these canonical songs set the stage for our friendship. They introduced us to one another without the need for speech.

They filled even those earliest days with dancing, raucous laughter, long-held memories cast across the room to cadences we knew by heart. Then came the impromptu ciphers: the entire crew circling up after a live event or while casually kicking back off-campus to craft verses from the information floating in the air all around us. I had been freestyling with Toya since I was four years old, though it was not something I shared with everyone. Besides the fact that you never know in advance exactly how a cipher experience is going to go (How good is the beatboxing? What is the mix of personalities in the circle? Is the environment around you conducive to spontaneous associations that are both situationally compelling and sufficiently witty to merit inclusion in the flow of things?) there is also, always, the question of decorum, and how to set the scene so the work can be made.

It was within this environment that I began to rediscover so much of what I remembered loving about performing in college on those CUPSI teams and with the Excelano Project. The crew in Coventry reminded me that what I needed from this time in my life, from these months spent living an ocean away from the only social world I had ever known, was to work as part of a collective, not only in my life as a writer and researcher but in every endeavor. I needed more ears, more eyes, on the stage-bound experiments I was putting together. If I pushed myself, I could compose new work every day. But the poems wouldn't be as strong, wouldn't take flight, without the critique and care of trusted friends.

Which brings me back to the G-Chat conversation that changed everything. A few months into my time in the UK, now freshly inspired by the artistic endeavors of my new-

found comrades, I went to my sister with an idea that was
still quite muddled but had something undergirding it that
felt genuinely electric. The basic premise of our recruitment
strategy would be simple: I would reach out to friends I had
made in the world of spoken word over the years, through
my youth slam days with Urban Word NYC and the Phila-
delphia Youth Poetry Movement, the College Unions Poetry
Slam Invitational, the Excelano Project, and, of course, my
time on the road. I would pitch them the basics of the idea
Toya and I had crafted, whole cloth, during that first con-
versation: "We are building a boutique arts agency that will
primarily represent poets working in the spoken word tradi-
tion. We'll put on shows as a collective, do photo shoots,
establish a social media presence, record videos of original
work, and then pitch that work year-round to middle schools,
high schools, colleges, universities, and corporations across
the country." This would be an opportunity for us to take our
individual and collective work more seriously—to take it to
another level of not only profitability but *polish*. The aim was
to elevate everything we did. Streamline it. And in the process
build a kind of life from poems that once lived only in the
archive of the air.

3.

I used one of my few allotted trips back home to see family
for Thanksgiving. During that trip, I made all the Strivers
Row phone calls over the course of two hours, and in no
particular order: Alysia Harris, Miles Hodges, Jasmine Mans,

and Carvens Lissaint. One by one, our team of poets agreed to come onboard. We got things started with a photo shoot in the neighborhood that inspired the name of our collective; one led by our fearless creative director, my brother-in-law, Marcus, who took beautiful photographs of us styled in vintage Harlem Renaissance–era attire. From there we set up a Facebook fan page for each individual poet and another for the entire collective. Then a group Twitter account and Strivers Row YouTube channel, both of which were maintained by Toya and Marcus. In the beginning, these online platforms were used to circulate already-existing videos of our performances, with the aim of expanding the potential real-world audiences for our live shows.

The performance footage and B-roll from those shows would eventually become the primary source of all our video content online. The driving force behind our marketing strategy was the idea that someone who was already a supporter of any one of us, or else simply enjoyed a viral video featuring our work that they encountered on another platform (or, as would later be the case, in their middle school, high school, or college classroom), might also appreciate the poems of another group member. In this way, we started the process of what we viewed as a sort of organic cross-pollination. What might begin as a connection with a single poem became an introduction to a wide range of poets in terms of aesthetics, politics, and literary influences.

This expansive, elaborate circuit was the direct outgrowth of Toya's larger vision. Which itself was an extension of both her experience as an events planner—before starting the company, she'd headed up the events division of a bridal magazine—and her familiarity with the spoken word scene internationally through our relationship over the years, especially my time in college as a poet who was often on the road. I ended up touring from my junior year forward at Penn, largely as a means of achieving economic independence and being able to save up so that I could take care of my family's needs as well as my own. This commitment was tested soon enough. My youngest nephew, Miles, was born on September 29, 2008, the same day that the stock market crashed. Several weeks later, Toya was out of a job. After a year or so of searching for a full-time position, we both decided that there had to be some way for us to help each other out. Following my performance at the White House in 2009, we had our chance. Gig requests came flowing in via Facebook and my personal email, and I had no idea of what I was supposed to do next.

From the very start, Toya's expertise made a difference. She had honed her eye for digital marketing while working in the magazine industry during her postgraduate years, and she brought those skills to bear in helping me build an online audience. Keep in mind that this was years before having a Facebook fan page or a YouTube channel was standard amongst writers. Toya found a gap in the marketplace and approached it brilliantly. In 2010, after a year of her managing me full-time, my first video went viral, for a poem, inspired by Jennifer Falu, entitled "10 Things I Want to Say to a Black Woman." It was, at its core, an ode to the black women in my life, and its list form gave it a structure that I returned to in the future:

1. I wish I could put your voice in a jar, wait for those lonely winter nights when I forget what God sounds like . . .
2. When I was born my mother's smile was so bright, it knocked the air from my lungs . . .
3. Who else could make kings out of us, turn a fatherless Christmas into a floor full of gifts and a kitchen that smells like the Lord is coming tomorrow and we must eat well tonight . . .

I heard news of the video's explosion in popularity from my friend Nana, who was also a record producer, MC, and sound engineer. Every time I refreshed the YouTube page, the numbers continued to spike. By the end of that first day, the video had amassed over a million views. That week, I received hundreds of friend requests on Facebook. I would eventually work with Nana and one of his close friends to film an HD version of the poem. That version, too, would go viral, and is the version of the poem that most folks recognize (though the video now available on YouTube was re-uploaded in 2011).

Once the 2010 HD recording of "10 Things I Want to Say to a Black Woman" reached a half million views, representatives from *The Mo'Nique Show* sent me a personal email inviting me to perform the poem live on the air. I was excited about the opportunity to share new work, but things changed rather quickly once we arrived at BET Studios. Unbeknownst to me, the show's producers had decided in advance that they wanted me to recite the poem in front of a live band. They thought, as one producer put it, that a viewing audience might "lose interest" in an a cappella version of the poem.

Seeing my discomfort, my sister jumped in immediately: "Cut the band or he doesn't go on." They did so without hesitation. I knew from that day forward that Toya should not only be my manager, but also manage other poets I knew and loved. We went home and talked about the idea in the kitchen, where we built out the vision from scratch. "It went from a moment to a movement," Toya says, "in that all of the arts experience I had and event experience culminated in this platform where people were not only coming to shows on campuses but then had this biannual event where they went through a whole transformation from watching you all online, individually, to seeing you onstage as a real collective."

From the very beginning, Toya said that our goal was to create *a new thing*: an arts-centered organization that didn't necessarily take the form of an arts-education-oriented non-profit like Urban Word NYC, or a venue like the Bowery or the Nuyorican, but a small group of artists and collaborators building something from the ground up, with all the best historical lessons from those sorts of spaces in mind. Toya was, and had always been, a poet. More precisely, she was a spoken word poet steeped in a long history of black institutions which held the literary and performing arts in high regard.

From pre-K through the sixth grade, Toya attended the Modern School in Harlem. Every year, they held a festival for the students where they had to learn songs in multiple languages (she remembers most vividly having to sing at the top of her lungs in French). After moving to Yonkers for middle and high school, she attended an HBCU, Hampton University, in Virginia, where she studied computer science and developed her skills as a poet. Toya read regularly at the local open-mic night, Fuzzy Wednesdays, and even started a poetry business where she wrote and sold pocket-sized love poems to her more bashful classmates.

But her relationship to the business, as well as her larger writing practice, began to change when she met her future husband and collaborator, Marcus, she says. Heartbreak had always been the engine of her creative output. Now, all her work as a writer and organizational leader would emerge from a different place: one rooted in a sense of community empowerment, collective responsibility, and abiding love. Their first date, she says, was six hours long. Marcus brought her to a local recording studio and played an album from one of her favorite underground artists. It turned out that he had been working on the album as an engineer. "Marcus was the kind of guy that would say, 'Oh, I heard this song. I bought a guitar. I'm going to play it. I'll practice it.' So, I always knew he had skills as far as music and sound." From the very start, the two were a formidable, in-house, creative team. Toya laid out an expansive social media plan before our very first show. Marcus had the idea that we should livestream the event, which in 2011 was so rarely done that Le Poisson Rouge (French for "the red fish"), the Greenwich Village venue hosting the show, didn't even have the technology on hand. A poetry and live music show we called *The Dean's List*—a performance featuring both solo and collaborative poems from each poet—was the venue's first-ever livestreamed event.

After the initial photo shoot and the creation of our requisite social-media accounts, we got to advertising for *The Dean's List*. This academic theme would go on to be a prominent one throughout our time together—*Anthology, Graduation*, et al.—as our audiences grew and our approach to the shows continued to expand. We invited just about everyone we knew to that first showcase: family members, colleagues from work, former adversaries who had come to appreciate the poetry, if nothing else. During the weeks when we publicized the event online and in person, we practiced tirelessly. I performed my poems from memory every single day in the weeks leading up to the show, reciting them over breakfast, at the laundromat, or during a morning run. For our inaugural set list, we decided that at least half of the poems we performed would be taken directly from our YouTube videos already in circulation; the other half would consist of work we'd written explicitly for the new show.

The first poem I planned to recite on opening night already had a video made for it, one that I had shot with a colleague, Olan Collardy, at the Naval College in London. Its title was "Balaenoptera": the genus of the blue whale. And though the poem entered the world of the Internet while I was in England, it had its roots as a piece of writing in my final days of undergraduate study at Penn, where, unbeknownst to me before my senior spring (though I'm sure someone must have mentioned it at some point), you had to take at least one class in the physical sciences, no matter your major, in order to graduate.

When my academic advisor, Janice Curington, shared the news with me, I was initially floored. For the next several days, I found myself poring through a softcover copy of the course list taken from the registrar's office, searching through unfamiliar disciplines to find a lifeboat. By the week's end, I had a plan: I would study oceanography. This realization was born, at the conscious level, from what I now recognize as a thoroughly unhelpful set of associations, largely based in my love of the oceanic as a site of literary and religious exploration: Noah's ark, *Moby-Dick*, Jonah and the giant fish, you get the general idea.

An introductory college course in oceanography, apparently, had nothing to do with my hard-earned expertise in maritime narratives. It didn't much help that our lectures took place on Thursdays in the late afternoon, which in my first year on tour was the window just before my flights out of Philly for weekend gigs at other colleges and universities. I was taking some of my first steps toward what would become something of a consistent question throughout my twenties— i.e., how to balance, in terms of both time and energy, my academic responsibilities with my love of the stage. With the help of generous professors, and fantastic academic advisors like Janice and Andrew Lamas, I put the pieces together. I even started to enjoy my oceanography lectures more and more, gradually discovering the poetry embedded within the science. What struck me most vividly, I remember, was a day in lecture when the professor told us that a blue whale *has a heart the size of a car*. The metaphor resonated with me. The biggest heart in the history of our planet. A love big enough to carry you inside of it.

With that image in mind, I sat down and wrote the poem those first weeks in England, letting the familiar art cut through newfound solitude:

When we are old, hair the color of tombstones, bones
that sound like wet windshield wipers whenever we
   slow dance through
the living room, I imagine I will look you in the eye.
   As if there is something small
and precious imprisoned there, say to you, darling, did
   you know
that a blue whale has a heart the size of a car? When
   you reply
correctly, as you always seem to do when I ask you
difficult questions about oceanography, I will probably
   just laugh.
Rejoicing over the fact that every time you smile, it
   makes the wrinkles
at the corner of your eyes look like six willow
   branches, all lifting
their heads from prayer in unison, the wind humming
   a somber hymn
beneath its breath just as our anthem jogs to a close.

Back home in New York a few weeks later, I would recite
this poem for the group in Shetler Studios, the now-shuttered
performance space where The Strivers Row held dress rehears-
als for every one of our shows. For at least two days in advance,
we would run the show from top to bottom, over and over,
workshopping the sequence of poems, musical accompani-
ment, and even individual lines, doing our best to polish every
aspect of the performance before it went live. "Balaenoptera"
represented a bit of a departure from both my more political
poems and my writing that was primarily focused on family,

but it was received well by my groupmates, and thoroughly edited at the level of performance through their feedback. What had only weeks before been a single, sprawling stanza in a Word document was now a story inscribed in muscle memory. I discovered, as my friend Carvens had shown me during our time performing together throughout my college years, how to "paint" the poem's imagery with my eyes, arms, and hands. When I invoked an hourglass big enough to hold the shoreline of every beach, I illustrated the scale of the device by gesturing to it at my side, measuring its height with my palms. The stars in the sky, more numerable than the grains of sand on Planet Earth, were pointed out one by one. In this way the poem came alive: via collective insight, purposeful movement, and embodiment through repetition.

On opening night at Le Poisson Rouge, the venue was packed to capacity. I was set to serve as the night's cohost alongside Carvens, which meant that we were both responsible not only for our poems, but also for remembering the sequence of poets, providing introductions for each member of the group, and keeping the audience energy up in between performances. I had never hosted a poetry show before, but I did once host a talent showcase sponsored by the National Association for Campus Activities (NACA) conference during my senior year of college. In addition to both crowd work and introducing the artists, I would share poems in the breaks between the magicians, singers, and comedy acts that took center stage to perform their work in front of hundreds of college students from across the country, hoping to get booked for campus gigs that would carry them through the year. Hosting a poetry showcase in NYC, especially one I had put together with my college friends and big sister, felt, at least at the outset, like it would demand a different, though related, skill-set.

Still, I wasn't too worried. I trusted Carv, and in my own strange way, also trusted the audience that we were now preparing to meet. If they had traveled from all over the city based on the promise of poems as interesting as the ones they had watched in their college dorm rooms, on the train to work, or else casually passing time in between errands, then I imagined I could trust them to hold me up as I figured out this new role. Plus, Carvens and I had known each other for three years before this most recent leg of our journey together as writers and collaborators. Our first face-to-face meeting was, of all places, at a poetry competition.

It was 2008. We had both signed up last-minute for an underground slam—it literally took place, every third week of the month, in the basement of a restaurant on the Lower East Side—and Carvens walked up to me before the event began. He'd just been named winner of the New York Knicks Poetry Slam a few weeks prior—"the Knicks Slam," as we called it, was a citywide youth poetry competition sponsored by the NBA team—and so I had some familiarity with his work. He mentioned that he had first heard my poems way back when I competed on the Brave New Voices slam team from New York in 2006, at age seventeen. New York had two teams that year, and I was on the one that lost in semifinals. I had also participated in the Knicks Slam that same year, which I won alongside four other youth poets from around the city (ours was the last year they named a group of five winners rather than just one).

Since then, I had gone off to college in Philadelphia, joined the Brave New Voices and CUPSI teams that won national championships in 2007, and come back to New York City several times for Thanksgiving, Christmas, and summer vacations, during which time I always found a way to return to the slam venues of my youth. Which is how I found myself, on this night, in a restaurant basement with little other than a modest speaker system, a stand-alone wired microphone and stand, and a crowd of people seated in foldable plastic chairs waiting for the event to get started. Carvens and I had both invited dates to this event for some reason (I'm hoping we can agree to chalk this regrettable choice up to the fact that we were teenagers), who met us there just after our brief introduction.

That night's event was billed as a "callout slam." To my knowledge, this kind of slam was invented in 2008, by an event organizer and spoken word poet named Kevin Benoit. The format of this newest category of slam was fairly straight-forward. You double the number of slam participants (four or five jumps to eight or ten) and have them pull cards with letters on them. The A card, naturally, goes first. Now, to clarify, this is also the case in more traditional slams. The difference in a callout slam is that before whoever pulled the A card gets up to perform, they "call out" one of the other poets in the audience. Those two poets will then be scored comparatively, head-to-head, with the lower-scoring poet being immediately eliminated.

Carvens was called out midway through the first full round of performances. In a stunner, he was eliminated after his first poem. With Carvens out, it was anybody's game. The smart money would have been on him, or a handful of other poets in the venue, to make it to the final round. By the end of the first, there were only two poets who had not yet been called out: myself and Marshall "Soulful" Jones, whom I had never seen perform live. I went first, and opted for a poem I can barely remember. The title, the content, it all blurs together for me now. But Soulful's performance was unforgettable. He recited a poem, from the first-person perspective, about the night several months prior when he had planned to die by suicide. During the long walk from his home, he heard raucous applause emerge from one of the buildings nearby. He walked inside, and witnessed a vision unlike anything he'd seen before: a Friday-night slam at the Nuyorican Poets Cafe. He stayed through the night of performances. In his own words, the poems he heard that night "saved his life." Soulful's poem, from beginning to end, was a meditation on hope, a reminder of the salvific power of a single line uttered aloud.

The crowd didn't *go wild*, exactly. It wasn't that type of performance. I don't recall yelling, or a round of snapping fingers. But there was applause throughout the venue, and a unanimous decision from the judges. In the last slot of the callout slam's first round, on the best winning streak of my life to that point, I had been knocked out. Reflecting on the slam a few months later, a mentor who heard the story secondhand would say, "You were trying to show off. Soulful spoke from a place that everyone could feel." From that day forward, my style, my approach to the craft, would never be the same. I would still throw in an occasional punchline or two. But the emphasis would always be on the human story, joy and pain. Falling short and overcoming.

After my unexpected early departure from the slam, my date and I thought it was best to leave. Carvens, whom I hadn't yet seen exit the restaurant, was right by the entrance to the venue. "That was a tough out," I offered, doing my best to add some levity that might temper our shared embarrassment, which at this point felt as if it had risen to the level of the catastrophic. He smiled. "We're gonna go grab some food. But it was good to meet you. Let's stay in touch." Carvens and I exchanged numbers, and we would continue to see each other at various slam and open-mic events throughout the city whenever I came back home. He quickly became one of my closest friends.

Having recently left college in upstate New York, Carvens decided around this time to give higher ed another try. But this time, he did so with the goal of pursuing a newly discovered passion: drama. He had never found a subject of study that truly called out to him up to that point, but Carvens discovered that he was an absolute natural on the actor's stage. He enrolled at the American Academy of Dramatic Arts in New York and upon his graduation (where he was also named the graduation speaker) studied acting at St. John's University in Queens. During our run with The Strivers Row, he would eventually be admitted, like Saul Williams, to NYU's Tisch School of the Arts. And that's not the only distinction he shares with Saul. Only months before our first show as a collective, Carvens would be named the Nuyorican Grand Slam Champion: the second-youngest poet to ever hold that title.

It was with all that history behind us that Carvens and I approached the task of hosting the first-ever Strivers Row showcase. Sound check and rehearsal that afternoon were uneventful in the way you hope for. The venue was gorgeous, each wall adorned in arrangements of red and violet lights that, in and against the omnipresent darkness of the underground space, gave off the sense that we were at some sort of postapocalyptic concert hall, participants in a subterranean fete celebrating the end of an era and the creation of something new. An hour or so before showtime, the line to get into Le Poisson Rouge wrapped around the block. Hundreds of people had come out on a Friday night in New York City to see us. Some, perhaps, had seen a single viral video on YouTube or Facebook. Others were friends from college, or else the New York youth poetry slam scene where Carvens, Miles, and I cut our teeth in our mid-to-late teens. Then there were those, we would gradually discover, who knew little or nothing about us as individual poets or even as a collective, but had seen our advertising online and thought they might as well check it out. At final count, there were 350 people packed in the venue for our first show.

Backstage, we gathered in a circle and prayed. Carvens and I ran onstage from the back to the sound of the live band and screaming crowd and got things going. Our emphatic introduction dovetailed into a night of performances that spanned the spectrum from love poems to a medley of R&B covers and original selections sung by guest vocalists to collaborative poems between multiple poets—what we call "group pieces"—that *also* included both the guest vocalists and the live band. It was a complete show. After that first night, we knew that we had something special on our hands.

After *The Dean's List*, the reach of the group only grew. We added a fifth member: Zora Howard, whose viral poem

"Biracial Hair" had been filmed the night we met, at the finals of the 2006 Urban Word NYC Youth Slam Finals.* We all saw an uptick in our social media followings, YouTube views, and requests to come perform on college and university campuses. Toya's vision was working: the students who came to our shows during summer and winter breaks went back to their schools and advertised on our behalf without prompting. Thus, we were able to create a vibrant ecosystem, a dynamic hybrid of online and live performance spaces. The live shows helped create the video content we distributed through You-Tube as well as our individual social media platforms (at the time, it was mostly Facebook, but we were also fairly early users of Twitter), while also allowing us to interface with the live audiences that would invite us to recreate our New York shows elsewhere.

Our approach to recording performances was like nothing else happening in the world of spoken word at that time. Marcus storyboarded every single one of our videos. Every shot used three cameras. You will see an audience shot, then a close-up, then another shot with a poet's hands and feet and facial expressions. As we'll see later, this wasn't the market-driven way to approach these sorts of videos. A single poet on a single microphone was the way to do things if you wanted to maximize the potential for online views. But that wouldn't have been true to form. The entire Strivers Row experiment, from the outset, was one born from a commitment to love

---

* Zora was also a member of the 2006 Brave New Voices youth team with me. In 2021, she was named a finalist for the Pulitzer Prize in drama for her play *STEW.*

and experimentation. There are videos of our early rehears-
als with my nephew, Toya's son, Miles, in the room, smiling,
watching the poems and songs. In a sense, he was the one
who inspired the creation of the company in the first place.
"The intention behind it," Toya recalls, "was really to also
save us. I had fought really hard to move to the company I
had moved to. I had my own office. Everything was going so
well. I thought, 'Great! This is success. This is what I've been
working for.' Then, when I was laid off shortly after return-
ing to work, The Strivers Row saved me in some way. I think
that was the real power of it—that it helped so many people.
I look at the impact it had on you guys," she tells me, "and
everyone's gone on to do great things. We didn't make a ton
of money from it, barely any money from it. But it was for
the culture, and it was for the artists."

Every element of The Strivers Row was, in truth, for the art-
ists. And not just the artists who worked under its aegis, but
the artists who made us possible, as well as the ones who
would come afterwards. It was a black-owned, family busi-
ness, but also a collective of black poets with a multicultural,
intergenerational, international audience. We were young
people trying to make our way in the world as students
and independent artists. This last part was not without its
drawbacks.

Take our UK tour, for example, in 2012. Leading up to it,
a friend of a friend offered to help us book our flights using
a connection they had to one of the airlines. We had already
set up all the venues, lodging, and ground travel for when

we landed. Supporters of the group were already purchasing tickets and letting us know via social media. Two months before the show, all lines of communication with the friend of a friend fell silent. They stopped answering calls, texts, emails. We soon realized that we had been tricked, and had no way of getting across the Atlantic at a rate we could afford for eight people. At the eleventh hour, Toya decided to call an audible: a fundraiser show to get money together for our plane tickets. We called it *Viewer's Choice*. A few weeks before the show, we set up a poll among all of our followers on social media, across platforms, to see what poems from YouTube they would like to see performed live. We returned to Le Poisson Rouge. We had a full house that night, and were able to pay for our tickets.

Once in England, we packed out two venues in London and another in Manchester, where JP Cooper, a singer we discovered through word of mouth and a few stellar clips of his music that were floating around online, opened the show. He also sang "Happy Birthday" to Toya. We returned to the States in one piece, and continued to tour as a group for the next four years. Collectively and individually, we would tour the US, the UK, India, Botswana, and South Africa several times over. We appeared on three seasons of TV One's television series *Verses & Flow*, alongside poets and musicians from across the world. We performed our final summer show in front of a sold-out, capacity crowd of 1,500 people at Stage 48 in Manhattan. Though we decided to stop touring together in 2015, by that point the group's impact on spoken-word poetry as both a discrete performance genre and a booming online business was evident. We had helped advance a certain approach to spoken-word performance in the digital age: a combination of livestreamed showcases of new material, social media presence, and the usage of traditional touring circuits (local slams, high schools, and college campuses). The members of the group eventually went off into different fields. As of this writing, two of us entered the worlds of film and stage drama, one went on to help found a media company, another edits a magazine dedicated to southern politics and culture, and one of us is an English professor who occasionally teaches classes on poetry and performance, where he gets to share videos of his friends and fellow travelers onstage, in front of a microphone, operating in their gifts. And talk about the world they made.

5.

Which leads us to the final point on the map: Button Poetry. Button is a hybrid YouTube channel and publishing house with over a million subscribers and tens of thousands of books sold each year. Its rise over the past eight years represents, in miniature, the future of the field; a truly singular moment within the spoken-word tradition. Founded by a group of poets and old friends in a St. Paul, Minnesota, living room, in 2011, the company has blossomed into an online juggernaut and influential publishing house. It has helped start the careers of any number of contemporary poets currently flourishing on the international touring scene as well in the world of literary publishing. What's more, Button has helped expand the audience of several poets who were already major players in the national slam scene, taking their work from an expansive network of local venues across the country out into the larger world: think here of Rudy Francisco, Sarah Kay, Phil Kaye, and Neil Hilborn, whose poem "OCD," on Button's YouTube channel, has over the past eight years become the most viewed spoken word poem of all time.*

I first heard about Button back in 2013, roughly two years into my life as a member of The Strivers Row. I followed a link one day to a video featured on Button's YouTube channel and was immediately impressed by the range of featured poets, the layout, and the sheer number of videos they had at their disposal (already, even then, numbering in the hundreds). I would come to find out that this library was the product of an underground approach to recording almost every high-profile spoken-word event happening in the country at a given time: the National Poetry Slam, the College Unions Poetry Slam Invitational, the Individual World Poetry Slam, the Rustbelt Poetry Slam, and the Women of the World Poetry Slam. Wherever poets were gathered for a festival or a competition, Button's cameras were there, in the audience, running from bout to bout, to commemorate the occasion. After doing some digging, I discovered that the company's founders were poets I had known for some years: Sam Cook, Michael Mlekoday, Sierra DeMulder, Dylan Garity, and Khary Jackson, all of whom I encountered for the first time through either a live poetry slam or YouTube footage of one of them performing.

Sam was the first member of the Button team I saw in real time. It was CUPSI 2009. The competition that year was held

---

* As of this writing, the poem has been viewed 15,608,738 times.

at my alma mater, the University of Pennsylvania. I heard the poet's name before I saw him—"Now coming to the stage, Sam Cook!"—and for a split second I almost expected a living copy of the late, great soul singer to walk onstage and belt out a classic record from memory. On this particular point, it bears mentioning that even though my mother and father's favorite singers, respectively, are Smokey Robinson and Stevie Wonder, I would imagine that Sam Cooke easily makes the R&B Mount Rushmore for both of them, as he held a place of genuine veneration in our home. Smokey and Stevie might have made the songs that meant the most to us individually, but everyone knew that Sam Cooke was in a class all his own as a vocalist. He had all the technical gifts in the world, and an urgency that shifted the entire atmosphere once you turned the record on. His chart-topping 1957 single "You Send Me" remains the most compelling musical shorthand I've ever encountered for how it feels to fall in love: "Darling, you send me."

The other Sam Cook* likewise had a voice that should shake a room. I don't remember the subject of his poem, but the uproarious crowd reaction it received is engraved onto my memory. I knew if the University of Minnesota team was starting off the bout with this poem, then it was one of their strongest (basic slam strategy states that you open with one of your most compelling poems, or poets). Sam was there to set the tone.

A decade after the bout, I got the chance to catch up with

---

* The version of the surname with an e attached was a stage name; the musical legend was in fact born on January 22, 1931, as Samuel Cook.

him again to talk about the history and impact of Button over the years. Much of what he had to say I had never heard before. But even the information I had already committed to memory Sam somehow enhanced with layers of detail that made the story of this small-midwestern-company-turned-global-influence feel new, and freshly compelling. Like the future of the genre was potentially even brighter, if infinitely more complicated, than I had imagined.

As it stands, the way vast numbers of young people on Planet Earth are encountering the genre of spoken word poetry is through the Button Poetry platform. The views and engagement data tell a story that's difficult to ignore: for over a decade now, millions of people have been exposed to the plurality of voices that make up the US poetry slam circuit via videos on Button's YouTube channel, which as of this writing boasts a subscriber base of 1.34 million. Many of the videos have also gone viral on platforms that are not YouTube: Facebook, Twitter, Instagram, TikTok, just to name the most prominent few. The company's effect not only on the way spoken-word videos circulate online, but on how a younger generation of poets now imagines and approaches the range of opportunities associated with poetry slam as such, is singular. I relay a version of this assessment of Button's influence to Sam at the start of our conversation, and his response is "What a thing to say out loud!"—which is both uniquely fitting given the subject matter at hand, and a reflection of the sense of wonder he still feels, even now, at the organization he and his collaborators created.

It all started in St. Paul, Minnesota. The initial cast of characters included Sam, Sierra DeMulder, Khary Jackson, and

Rachele Cermak. Outside of their role in the founding of Button, this group is notable for the fact that in 2009, representing the Soap Boxing Slam in St. Paul, they brought home the city's first National Poetry Slam title. They then went on to repeat as national champions in 2010. After the second nationals win, the Soap Boxing poets were invited to perform at college campuses and local slam venues across the country. During that second year on tour, over the course of an ordinary, if somewhat stressful, drive from St. Paul to Kalamazoo, Michigan (a trip made necessary by the fact that the student group that booked them for the show had forgotten to book their plane tickets), something clicked. Somewhere in the first half of that eight-hour drive, while debating ways to build a system that was a bit more sustainable than the one that had led them to this point, the group had an epiphany: "We're scraping by, trying to make a living doing this and doing shows and touring," Sam recalls. "We're in the car and I'm pitching this whole vision of how we build a system that'll make this sustainable. How do we survive in this for more than five years? Where are the resources? How do we add some resources?" From this series of questions emerged the earliest conception of what would eventually become Button's YouTube channel. He explains: "Back then, the goal was to distribute burned CDs. It's one of the funniest little bits of the whole arc that when we first started, we're trying to link together midwestern slams—Detroit, Columbus, Minneapolis or Minneapolis–St. Paul, Omaha, and either St. Louis or Denver. We were trying to put five of those six into a group and have all five slams contribute to a quarterly burned CD that would have all the poets on it. And all the slams would get it for free in exchange for helping contribute content. So in all five cities you'd have a little bit of an audience. You'd use the CD as prizes at your slam. You'd sell it at fundraisers. That was the original goal, and we literally could never get five cities to put their heads together. We were selling books on five continents before we'd get five slams to negotiate this burned CD, and so I never actually achieved the initial goal of Button, but that's what it was: to make a more beautiful product."

These earliest visions of Button, then, can be described as an extension of work that was already happening on the ground in the Midwest, and with a fair amount of regularity elsewhere in the country. The core of the plan was, simply, to connect people; to bring together a small group of midwestern poetry slam venues and create a collaborative product that could then be used to help keep the lights on. This version of Button's process met with various difficulties early on, and ultimately flamed out before it could even get started in earnest. Rather than be deterred by this early failure, the Soap Boxing crew chose to make the pivot from a strictly audio approach to one that would emphasize video—this, they thought, would not only better circulate the social wealth of the midwestern slam scene, but indeed bring the vibrancy of the slam scenes all over the world to an audience that otherwise would not know they existed. In Dylan Garity's words, Button was initially "a merch idea": a way to help artists have more professionally produced merchandise that they could sell at poetry slams or shows on the road. He describes to me a familiar scene: you've just come offstage, and someone says that they enjoyed your set. You can tell that they mean it, not only from the look in their eyes and the tone of their voice, but because they ask where you will be performing next, and if you have any merch, usually CDs or a chapbook.

Asking for merch in the slam context can be understood, on one level, as simply an expression of a desire to spend more time with the work of the artist you have just discovered. But I tend to think there's another element to it. Given the sheer speed with which so much spoken-word merch, historically, has been put together—a CD burned at your friend's house earlier that afternoon, a chapbook hot off the printer at the Staples around the corner—my sense has always been that these exchanges are primarily about *support*; a way for audience members to feel like they are contributing to the livelihood of the person who has just moved them onstage. Button's aim was to find a way to streamline that process and make things easier for both the poet and the listener/supporter: more time on the writer's side to focus on the work, and a better product at show's end for the listener.

Most of this initial brainstorming took place in Sam's living room. There, the crew regularly assembled to toss around ideas for the business, but also to engage in philosophical ruminations on what spoken word as a genre meant to them in the first place, what it could become, what it could accomplish in the world. They would write and edit poems as a group. Sam also had two house cats, interfering with and participating in the process in the most charming ways possible. Dylan would come up from the Twin Cities, where he'd arrived in 2008 to study at Macalester College, with friends and colleagues to think alongside the group, workshop ideas, and engage in the outreach necessary to try to turn the Midwest poetry slam mixtape idea into a reality. He described it as witnessing something akin to a "generation of performance there," seeing not only the other founding members in their element, but the younger poets who had been coached by them over the years. It was in this space that the mixtape idea—which started out as little more than a side project, where the group would burn a hundred or so CDs featuring midwestern poets, and then divide them up between slam masters in Chicago, Madison, Minneapolis, et al.—eventually gave way to the essence of what Button would one day become: a curated site for spoken word on an international scale.

Dylan had already, during his college days, spent hours upon hours filming the Macalester poetry slams, editing that footage, and posting it online. He eventually noticed that similar videos of spoken-word performances from CUPSI and elsewhere—dozens of them, in fact—were spread over an equal number of individual YouTube channels. Few of these channels were spoken-word-themed in any meaningful way, but rather were accounts managed by friends and loved ones of the poets, or else by people who were fans of the art more generally. There were very few spaces online where you could consistently find spoken-word poems, outside of a handful of regional channels that produced live shows on a weekly basis, and would feature every poem performed at the venue that week.* You had to know where to look. As it stood, hundreds

---

* One of the most prominent examples of these channels is speakeasynyc, which, as of this writing, has almost 150,000 subscribers and features writers from across the US when they come to perform in New York City venues.

and hundreds of poems recited at slams over the years were living on primarily through grainy phone-camera footage, VHS tapes gathering dust in someone's garage, or else only in memory, gradually fading from view as a generation of these performers, as well as their in-person audiences, grew older.

The ephemerality of a given poem lent real, palpable urgency to its moment of utterance. In witnessing it live, you were seeing something no one had ever seen performed precisely this way, in front of this crowd, under these blazing lights. You were experiencing a work of art that no one ever would again. Button's approach doesn't undermine the raw truth of this experience, though it certainly complicates it. With a Button camera in the room, you can relive these poems whenever you want. They might be worse than you remember, or better. The video might bring you back to a space you would rather recall only in the haze of reverie. It might reveal something you missed. There is also the fact that much of what is performed at open mics is, quite often, simply not very good. This, of course, is entirely the point. An open mic is intended to be a space for amateurs, for artists trying out new material, as well as those who have never stepped onto a stage in the first place. It is a place to grow, and fail, and be transformed. This also means that footage from open mics, and any number of local slams, is not representative of the strongest work produced in the field. Constant, high-level curation would be Button's contribution to the genre.

For Sam, the move from burned CDs to video footage also had a fair amount to do with his childhood environment. Long before he found poetry slam, he was being raised by a family with a real love of cinema, and a serious commitment to the idea that videography could be used as a force for good in the world. This larger vision had a marked influence on Sam. From the very beginning of his spoken-word career, even when he was touring full-time and trying to make a living from it, a deep consideration of the cinematic element of things, as well as the politics of the work itself, was always there. He was always recording. At first, exclusively on the two-hundred- and three-hundred-dollar cameras he purchased at local stores in St. Paul. But once the idea for the company that would eventually become Button came to him, he knew he would need new equipment to deliver the more beautiful product he saw in his dreams. After two years on the road together, the touring collective broke up. Sam and Dylan remained close. More than that, they remained committed to the project of recording spoken-word performances around the country on their own dime. They started locally, working with students at places like Carleton College to record poetry videos. This was highly produced live footage of poets essentially wandering through the city reciting their work. Initially, there was an argument that this could be the core content of the channel. Eventually, Sam and Dylan decided to apply for a Verve grant from Intermedia Arts—a Twin Cities arts nonprofit, now defunct, that was founded in 1973. Sam and Dylan's application was successful, and Intermedia Arts awarded them several thousand dollars to buy a new camera.

New equipment in hand, Dylan and Sam began flying across the US to record the biggest poetry slams of 2013 and 2014: CUPSI, WOWPS, and NPS. At the time, Sam was also the coach of the Macalester College CUPSI team, and started to shoot new footage whenever the team would compete. Wherever hundreds of poets were gathered, he found a way to be there, right at the front, trying to get as much footage as humanly possible for the archive. From his perspective, it wasn't necessarily about views or revenue yet. The ethos was simply to follow the work wherever it led. Every competition that could be reached would be filmed, and the strongest footage of the strongest poems would go online. Between 2012 and 2013, the first fifty videos went up on the Button Poetry channel. In the spring of 2013, several of the videos—like Javon Johnson's "cuz he's black," a Baldwinian letter to his nephew where he reminds him, at the edge of tears, that black Americans "don't have the luxury of playing war / when we're already in one"—began racking up hundreds of thousands of views.* At this point, Sam and Dylan were working twenty to thirty-five hours a week on curating content. The channel only grew from there.

For the Button founders, it eventually became clear that the company had a potential which exceeded the world of live-performance footage. So the group turned to one of the original living room poets, Michael Mlekoday, to develop and direct their publishing arm. There were already a few other small presses primarily focused on spoken-word poets at the time—namely, Penmanship Books and Write Bloody Books—and the sense among the group was that they had something unique to contribute to that already flourishing landscape. Starting off with a chapbook contest in 2012, But-

---

* A number of the other videos can still be found on Button's YouTube channel. Some, like "cuz he's black," now boast views in the millions.

ton would build an impressive lineup of authors over the next few years, many of whom had their big break as poets featured in viral Button videos.

Michael paints an ornate, sprawling picture not only of those earliest days in the living room, but of an entire social scene of midwestern poets and poetry slams that served as the soil from which Button eventually sprang: "There was this broader sense of community and exchange between the slams in Wisconsin, Minnesota, Chicago, to some degree Nebraska, considering Omaha can fit in there sometimes," Michael says. "And then most of our featured poets, before we had nationally famous slam poets who were touring the country because they had books or videos on YouTube, were from other midwestern cities."

This constellation of local venues and individual voices, slam scenes and regional sounds, constitutes a cartography quite unlike that which we might normally associate with the history of spoken word: Minnesota, Wisconsin, and Nebraska. Later on in our conversation, Michael will invoke Detroit and the truly astonishing number of poets that have emerged from that city over the years who both competed in poetry slams and went on to shine in the world of literary publishing and academia: not just Tyehimba Jess, but Airea D. Matthews, Jamaal May, and Vievee Francis, the list goes on and on. Theorizing the history of spoken word *from the middle* in this way aligned powerfully with my own thinking about the fact that even though poetry slam was notably *invented* in the Midwest, it is often now associated with dominant slam teams, venues, and individual poets on either coast. Early on, Button's work—and not just that of its founders, but that of most of the poets featured on its channel—was an exercise in an expansive group of young midwestern poets defining themselves over and against such an impulse. Button wasn't the only game in town on this front. There was also the Midwest Slam League, which would set up a series of poetry slams in different midwestern cities throughout the year, all preceding the national competition. This helped produce a distinct sense of camaraderie, Michael says, when one of the St. Paul teams would end up at NPS and see a team from Milwaukee that they had just competed against earlier in the year in a bout against them and a team from Austin, another from Philly, another from New York. There was this feeling, unspoken but deep, that they were in it together, even in a moment of competition. Michael also mentions poets I've known since I was a teenager: Will Evans and Ed Mabrey over in Columbus, Ohio, for example, both of whom played a major role in bringing that scene to national prominence. Through this network of regional slams, each with its own voice and practices and protocols, the sort of in-person connections that would make Button a distinct force in the digital world were first forged.

Depending on whom you ask, the major turning point for the organization came at the Women of the World Poetry Slam in Austin, Texas, in 2014. That was the first time that the crew set out to film a tournament with multiple cameras moving between disparate rooms, bouts, and poets. Sam recounts a tale of running at breakneck speed from venue to venue—first the True Love Café, then the Spider House— with his newly purchased thousand-dollar camera in hand, trying to make sure he captured the strongest performances of the night. He describes sprinting through the front door into the Spider House while sweating from head to toe, just in time to see the poet he had planned to film already a minute and a half into her poem, much too late to get usable footage for the YouTube channel. This was a common issue in those earliest years of Button: Sam had been here before, feeling this exact same disappointment, numerous times, in various venues across the country. But there was a piece of feedback he received in that moment, he says, that altered the way he approached the business from that day forward. Suzi Q. Smith, a poet from the Denver slam venue, Slam Nuba, looked a visibly haggard Sam up and down and said, "You really care about this. We've worked with a lot of people, and you're doing all this for free." This was the moment, this briefest conversation, when Sam knew that he and the rest of the Button crew had something special. Someone he counted as a pioneering voice in the genre recognized that the work they were doing mattered, and that this might be the missing piece in the link between spoken-word performance and the audience of millions the form was made for. He had an epiphany that night: "the desire is there, the audience is there, and I have the skills to connect the two." It was the hardest he had ever worked at anything. And more importantly, he knew that the content was strong. With well-shot poems, each performed at the sort of heights that high-stakes competition often elicits, there were no limits on what they could build.

The strategy was straightforward enough: take a simple front or side shot of the performance—no panning of the camera, no music or visual effects—and edit it into a video that includes the title of the poem and the name of the poet.

Close with the Button logo and a link to other videos. Repeat. Understandably, this was a real source of conflict among a number of Button Poetry collaborators. One argument was that each video should be treated as an occasion for robust collaboration, with the poets involved at every step of the editing process. Another was that there should always be a high production value and certain level of polish to anything they uploaded to YouTube.

There was a trial-and-error approach in the early Button days that yielded mixed outcomes: attempts at poetry mix-tapes and highly stylized short films built around individual poems failed to produce the sort of traffic that the more straightforward videos did. The more involved approach also demanded a higher cost in terms of labor hours for the small, dedicated team. Some of it, too, was simply a recognition of the common strength of most spoken-word artists they worked with: the performance of a given poem in the moment—not a track recorded in a studio with multiple takes and ad-libs, or a video shot over the course of many hours. The primary focus of the channel would be the production of videos that captured the *immediacy* of spoken-word performance; its undeniable intensity when shared with a crowd for the first time. "What we want to do is create the experience of being in the room," Sam says. "We want the camera to be transparent. We want the camera to allow you to feel like you're in the room. We don't want to show the camera. This is about the poem and the poet. Get the camera and the videographer out of there. They're not important. They're not the stars. We rolled back, and I pushed and pushed and pushed until I had a team and a successful system that was simple, dressed down, elegant, beautiful, high-quality, and really about removing any kind of barrier between the poem, the poet, and the audience."

Talking to the founders of Button, the ethos became more clear to me. All these young people spent years in rooms where this work was being created, start to finish, in real time. Their gambit was that if they could even come close to replicating that experience digitally, people watching online would be impacted the way they had been as younger poets, just starting out. That they would instantly fall in love with the form. All it would take was a steady hand to let them see and hear the poet as clearly as possible.

When asked why this model had been so successful, though, the message I received had less to do with these particular aesthetic choices than it did with a certain set of ideas about the spirit of our cultural moment. Even with their shortcomings, spoken-word performance venues have always made room for those seeking the opportunity to share their ideas, their unfinished dreams, and be recognized; these spaces are open fora in which a more robust language for our joy, our fear, our loneliness and unabashed awe can be crafted in community. In a world that was continually speeding up, streamlining, elevating its pace even as we all grew more isolated from one another, and from the social practices that make an art form like spoken word possible, there remained a need for emotional revelation.

The response to this model has been nothing short of astonishing: Button Poetry has accumulated just over twelve hundred years of watch time since the channel started. Hundreds of thousands of people across the world are encountering the artists whose work is featured there. They are memorizing the poems, getting tattoos of their favorite lines, and going to live shows to support the poets they discover through the channel. Throughout the early years of Button, there was also a public, live-show component in St. Paul: Button Poetry Live. A fair amount of the channel's early content are videos taken directly from these events, which featured guest poets from around the country performing alongside regulars from within the spoken-word community in St. Paul. Between 2013 and 2018, Dylan traveled back and forth between St. Paul and Los Angeles—where he was pursuing independent writing projects alongside his work at Button—before moving back to the Twin Cities for two and a half years to help the company grow. He left Button Poetry officially in 2018. Michael left a year or so later to pursue a PhD in English from the University of California, Davis. Sam is still the company's president, and the sole member of the founding group who has remained. The organization has a full-time staff and is based, as ever, in St. Paul.

During the early weeks and months of the COVID-19 pandemic, the need for avenues like Button and its unique influence in the spoken-word space became evident to me in a new way. And not just Button, but the interfaces in which it lives: the Internet, the screen, whether it's in a smartphone or a laptop or a desktop in the high-school computer lab. Increasingly, in a moment when any number of world-famous venues are either closing or in danger of closing, there is the persistent sense that this might become the way most young people encounter the genre itself, well into the future. What does it mean to rely on this sort of digital space to approximate, however beautifully, something one might never encounter in the flesh, in the room where not only the poems but the laughter, the whispers, the roar and applause of the crowd, are all also part and parcel of what you remember months afterward as *the performance*?

Without the gathered assembly, no spoken-word poem achieves airspeed. There is a specific set of rituals in St. Paul, at the Soap Boxing Slam. There is a certain way of doing things that is distinct at the Mercury Cafe in Denver, the Cantab Lounge in Cambridge, the Rotunda in West Philly. Or in Union Square, at Bar 13. At the Nuyorican, we would all get up and dance to Bell Biv DeVoe before the slam got started. It would have made little sense to say that this ritual, this announcement, movement, and song, was truly ancillary to the poets and poems that followed, the way that they could shake you and everything you knew. It was all inextricably bound up together.

In one way, the Button formula does approximate the fleeting moments in slam's live venues: it only ever captures a single performance of a single poem. Even when there might be a range of recordings of live performances of a certain poem out there, the one that blows up on Button's channel, the one that reaches that audience and from there the world, ends up representing the single, definitive performance of it. Naturally, there are drawbacks and benefits to this reality. On the one hand, the Button rendition of a given poem might not be your best. It might not be the version of your work that you would hold up as the most elegant or true expression of who you are as an artist. But there's something to the idea that each of these poems becomes a kind of time capsule, holding its truth about the moment in which it was spoken, especially for young poets just starting out. A reminder of a time where the poem, the stage, were at the very center of your life and, for even a brief moment, the central focus of attention of hundreds, thousands, millions of people. The videos crystallize that connection. They keep it within an archive you can return to with the click of a button.

The relationship between these forms of exchange—the slam performance that becomes a viral video that becomes a book—is still, of course, unfolding. We are yet in the midst of an entirely new generation of writers who began their literary careers in the realm of competitive spoken-word performance and, more specifically, in a world that has been chronicled by Button *in real time* over the past decade. Even before COVID, several of the major poetry-slam organizations began collapsing: PSI and CUPSI most prominently. We are seeing the dissolution of any number of regional and indie slams that once flourished. Even as the videos continue to proliferate online, and more and more spoken-word poets score book deals, literary awards, and TV and film credits, the venues that gave birth to the format are transforming. Which leaves an open question for us to consider: what's the next format, the next iteration, the next vision for spoken word? The hunger is clearly still there. The audience is larger than ever. But where will the work find its sustaining life force, its source of renewable energy?

That aspect of the art form's future remains opaque. But what is clear is that for people like Sam, the ethos of paying artists for their time, and trying to help people find a way to feed themselves from the proceeds of the art they create, remains paramount. "This has been my only job for coming on almost a decade now," he says. "I think it's seven years, something like that. But I've never taken any profit out of this company. . . . I don't know if that matters or not, but I think it's important to acknowledge that that's not what this is. Sometimes I talk to people and they think that there's a lot of cash in the back end of Button, that we're making a ton of money. We pay salaries. We pay people. We pay artists. If you appear on our stage for an event outside of the slam, then you get paid. Every single person. I believe in that, and that's maybe stupid. When I talk to financial advisors they say, 'You don't understand business.' I say, 'We disagree on business.'"

What sort of ethical relationships does an institutional enterprise built from poems, from public acts of passionate utterance, demand? What should their character be? For the founding members of both Button and The Strivers Row, it always came down to finding ways to help people build lives for themselves and their loved ones. Not only compensating the poets for their time and labor, but helping them create works that could travel with them for years on end and help them pursue other opportunities in the future. It came down to friends in rooms, trying to build something bigger than they had ever seen before. "I took no small amount of inspiration from y'all in Strivers Row," Sam told me. "I mean, you guys were out there doing the thing before we were, making it look great. . . . I remember watching your videos and hanging out and thinking, 'Man, these guys are really doing it. How do we figure out what they're doing?'"

—

And so the tradition continues, from living room to living room. From a small group of twentysomethings gathered at a friend's home, taking buses and planes back and forth between Los Angeles and Minneapolis and St. Paul, packing boxes with books to ship out to the customer as quickly as possible from the two-room office in downtown Minneapolis that became the four-room office in downtown Minneapolis filled with hundreds of books and two computers for editing. From a conversation about mix CDs in a car on an eight-hour drive to Kalamazoo, to millions of views and careers built from a moment onstage now set in the amber of Internet acclaim and a singular archive of spoken-word footage, a seemingly endless engine, sending thousands of poems out across the world on a daily basis. In all sorts of ways, Button's trajectory has helped shape the trajectory of the genre more broadly. Through public-facing programs like its online video contest, hundreds of poets from around the globe have been able to share their original work. The only requirement? That the poems be audible. You don't need a professional crew, or a two-thousand-dollar camera. Just the sound of your own voice, and the confidence to send your words off into the unknown.

I am reminded in my conversations with the Button founders that slam was built on the idea that everyday people—quite literally, a random group of five judges in a given venue—are the ones who should decide what constitutes moving, meaningful poetry. They believed that expertise, or at minimum good taste, was generally dispersed throughout the population, and could be regularly found in the kind of people who might gather to hear poems on a Wednesday night. The expansion of those hundreds of small rooms—the bars, lounges, auditoria, and cafes that give this genre life all over the Earth—into the world of the Internet took this premise to its very limits. Then, as now, it was never just about the scores. The competition is an excuse for the people to get together. Now there are simply more of us in here, millions more, than we ever could have imagined.

Spoken word, these conversations remind me, removes the distance between us. It brings the writer and reader face-to-face. Rather than the book, or the sentence, or the written line being the unit of transmission, it is the human voice of the authors themselves, right there in front of you, saying, "I wrote this. I memorized this, and agonized over it, and practiced it for hours, including during the walk here, for the express purpose of sharing it with you." Now we've built this unwieldy machine together. Consciousness to consciousness, against the threat of the ticking clock. That experience is made available to millions of human beings every time a new video goes up. To firefighters and construction workers and engineers and nurses and dancers and mail handlers. And to English teachers anxious about the upcoming poetry unit, who just want to show their students that there are writers, dead and living, who look like them, and understand their concerns. There will always be new approaches to this craft we love. The next generation of poets will engineer a version of this art form that is unique to them, and thus in many ways unfamiliar *by necessity.* Having come, as all transformative art does, from the future.

Epilogue in Three Parts:

The Hill We Climb, Summertime,
A Few of My Favorite Things

I think it's somewhere about the fourth or fifth grade when we learn to see the written word as a different entity from the spoken. This detracts from our ability to stay in touch with the fact that the spoken word is a physical entity that is as solid as this table and has its own laws. If it's true that as I'm talking to you bones are moving in your inner ears, I'm physically touching you with my voice.

—Etheridge Knight

For the more or less brief time the poem lasts, it has a specific and unmistakable temporality, it has its own time.

—Giorgio Agamben

What if our political strategy began from the question: what do children need?

—Joy James

The Hill We Climb

The morning of the inauguration, my wife and son and our family dog, Apollo 5, and I are in the living room, eating snacks on the big gray couch. It is midday, and I've heard through the grapevine earlier in the week that poetry is scheduled to make its return to the White House lawn. The most recent performances of this kind, by Elizabeth Alexander and Richard Blanco, respectively, were already etched into my memory. But I read in passing—this part had somehow eluded the online rumors I had come across thus far—that today's long-awaited ceremony would feature an *emerging* poet, rather than an established figure within the field.

Admittedly, I arrived to the televised stream of the inauguration in medias res, having just put final touches on an earlier section of the book you are now holding. It turns out I was just in time. The bright-yellow coat was what first caught my eye—an ideal choice, I thought, for the moment (every poem, as you now know, begins before you step onstage). But it was the power and precision of the recitation that kept my attention. Both the singularity of the occasion—Amanda Gorman was the youngest poet, by many years, to have her original poem featured at an inauguration—and the echoes of performances past stood out immediately.

The cultural impact of Gorman's inauguration reading was immediate. In it, we heard a poet with a fantastic ear for internal rhyme, alliteration ("we will raise this wounded world into a wondrous one") and assonance ("we did not feel prepared to be the heirs / of such a terrifying hour"). We also bore witness in her performance style—the cadence, the hand gestures—to the influence of luminaries such as Patricia Smith, Miguel Algarín, Sunni Patterson, Saul Williams, and so many others. The National Youth Poet Laureate program from which Gorman emerged has its roots in the work of Urban Word NYC, an arts organization in Manhattan that has long been a proponent of youth poetry slam, as well as a launchpad for poets committed to both the page and the stage. Gorman's performance, then, comes to us in the present as a powerful example of what can happen when a culture embraces the literary imagination of young people, and helps equip them with the tools to explore their gifts in community. She represents a reflection of what generations of spoken word poets envisioned and worked toward in different ways: the intersection of a robust commitment to the dance of language on paper and the singular power of poems given to the air.

In subsequent interviews, Gorman doesn't self-identify as a spoken-word poet. The genre, it seems, has had such a meaningful impact—and this is thanks as well, I think, to national programs like Poetry Out Loud, which encourages the study and recitation of poems from an expansive array of writers and traditions—that the kind of cadence and body language we might once have expected to see only from someone trained in the world of poetry slam is now ubiquitous within communities dedicated to the poetics of public speaking. Both Gorman's performance at the inauguration and the body of work she produced in the time shortly thereafter—a book-length version of the inaugural poem, a debut collection of poetry, and a recorded performance featured at the Super Bowl—were clearly aimed at the cultivation not only of a larger audience for poetry, but of what felt like a new audience altogether.

The resonance of "The Hill We Climb," then, as a moment of public oratory, is multiform. As a matter of protocol, it signaled the return of the literary and performing arts to the White House, after four years where they were absent. It was a moment of pride in what was still possible here, living in this especially harrowing stretch of the long historical experiment we share. But in an entirely different vein, Gorman's performance served as a striking reminder that in a moment when so many poetry organizations geared toward adults were either in disarray or already collapsed, young people were willing and able to lead the genre in a new direction. To be the public face of the art form and represent it at a high level: with poise, clarity, and singular focus.

Gorman hails from Los Angeles and was raised with her twin sister, Gabrielle (now a filmmaker) in the Watts section of the city by her mother, Joan Wicks, who is an English teacher. She says she was raised with little exposure to television and spent a fair amount of time in those early years immersed in the world of books and honing her love of writing. This passion for intense study and creative praxis alike was not only manifested in Gorman's home life, however. Years before she worked with the National Youth Poet Laureate program, she was a member of WriteGirl, a nonprofit literary-arts organization in Los Angeles dedicated to creating writing opportunities in fiction, poetry, screenwriting, journalism, and several other genres for teenage girls and nonbinary youth. WriteGirl provides one-on-one mentoring for over five hundred young people through its programs; 100 percent of its graduates have attended college over the past decade-plus. After high school, Gorman would go on to attend Harvard University, where she studied sociology, and graduated in 2020.

Back in ninth grade, Gorman was a new mentee in the WriteGirl program alongside her twin sister. In her own words: "It's been thanks to their support that I've been able to chase my dreams as a writer." Gorman's invocation of a literary arts organization as a primary pillar of support during her journey is instructive. Like so many of the writers whose lives animate the pages of this book, her story is not simply one of individual skill or brilliance, but one of greatness discovered, honed, through collective practice and an emphasis on writing in community. "The hill we climb" turns out be an apt metaphor indeed. The beauty of the journey is in collective striving. Any peak we reach, any knowledge gained from the view up there where the light seems to shine down just a little bit brighter, is made all the more meaningful by the fact that it is held in common. We persist for the sake of one another. We climb so that we might see the world more clearly.

Summertime

Carlos López Estrada did not discover spoken word through a literary arts organization. Nor through a Wednesday-night poetry slam or an open mic downtown. Estrada found the craft, not unlike those earliest progenitors of the contemporary spoken-word sound, through his friends. Before he became someone who makes movies, groundbreaking ones like *Blindspotting* and *Summertime*, he made music videos. This was how he first got linked up with Daveed Diggs, who at the time was splitting his days between a star-making Broadway debut in *Hamilton* (pulling double duty, famously, as both Thomas Jefferson and the Marquis de Lafayette) and being the lead MC of the avant-garde hip-hop group, clipping. Diggs, who hails from Berkeley, California, is also an alumnus of Brave New Voices. During his days as a student at Berkeley High, spoken word was simply a part of his everyday routine: "It was woven in the fabric of the community. I don't think I realized how special that was until I left. I didn't know that it wasn't part of what everyone did when they were teenagers, which was to go watch your friends spit poems."[1]

This much-longer history is evident in Estrada's first film, *Blindspotting*, which features both Diggs and his longtime friend and colleague, Rafael Casal, another Brave New Voices alumnus (his San Francisco team won the youth title in 2004). Estrada's debut features spoken word performances at several key junctures, most often in moments of great duress involving the criminal-justice system. The central character that Diggs plays, Collin, is on probation, a fact that becomes a kind of narrative device, driving the action forward (there is, quite literally, a probation countdown that marks the passage of time throughout). In *Blindspotting*, the first of these moments of conflict with the carceral state takes place in the world of dreams: a courtroom nightmare is one of the film's standout set pieces, and the place where Casal, in the role of Collin's ne'er-do-well best friend, Miles, gets to showcase his talents as a poet. Another transpires in the real world, in the film's denouement, where Diggs recites a spoken-word piece as a means of confronting the police officer he saw kill an unarmed black man only days before—"did you count his rings when you bled him / when you dead him / how old was he / how old was he—." As much as the film is centrally concerned with the psychological toll of Collin witnessing this event, the social catastrophe of gentrification in Oakland, California, and the need for a radically new vision of law enforcement and the pursuit of justice, it is also a movie about Collin and Miles's bond. About freestyling with a friend after you get off work, drama with family members, watching all your relationships grow more complex with age.

Estrada's second film, *Summertime*—which debuted to positive reviews at the Sundance Film Festival in 2020—retains a measure of its predecessor's political edge, but is mostly marked by its emphasis on the myriad difficulties, and ineliminable joys, of being young in the present day. It follows a group of twenty-five teenage poets around the city for an unspecified amount of time, cataloguing their trials, tribulations, and moments of transcendence: their desire for hip-hop-industry fame, respect at work, and love. Standard dialogue in the film is interspersed with spoken-word poems that genuinely jump off of the screen: an overheard homophobic comment on a bus is confronted with a queer love anthem from a teenage girl babysitting two children; the counter of a fast-food restaurant turns into a stage for poetry and social rebellion; a street-corner MC duo named Anewbyss and Rah go from relative obscurity to the top of the charts. Here, summertime is setting and subject and narrative device: an alchemical force that blurs moments, minutes, months of action within the course of a ninety-five-minute film. There's also the fact that the poems in the film are treated as poems. They are not breaks in the flow of standard narrative. People clap afterwards. They shed tears. They stop and stare in astonishment. In allowing this original work, composed in collaboration with the teen poets of Get Lit, a Los Angeles–based youth arts organization, to stand on its own, Estrada makes yet another startling intervention into the tradition of spoken word cinema. *Summertime*, after all, is not a documentary, or else a gritty drama about the difficulties of being a poet on the contemporary scene. It's a film, shot over seven months with handheld cameras on a modest budget, about life as it is lived for this distinct group of young people in Southern California. The poems are merely meant to bridge the gap between the mundane and the inexpressible, allowing the film's multiple protagonists to do what so many of us wish we could do in a moment of conflict or great difficulty: to stop time, if only for a second; to be the clearest, most courageous, most eloquent version of ourselves when the occasion calls for it. *Summertime* allows us to live in the fullness of such a dream—and to linger there for as long as we need.

A Few of My Favorite Things

Just about every single one of my son's play uncles and aunties is a professor or a preacher, a visual artist or a self-taught poet—some are several of these at once—which means that alongside the adorable ultramarine bucket hat and embroidered blankets he received as his earliest gifts, even before he was born, there was a veritable multitude of books. The offerings spanned a wide spectrum. There were classic works (*Corduroy*; *Oh, Kojo! How Could You!*) and more recent additions to the canon of children's literature (*Ellington Was Not a Street*; *Life Doesn't Frighten Me*). Some were meant to help him fall asleep, others to raise his awareness of his people's place in history and their indelible role in shaping the present day. It was no small matter, I soon realized, the process of choosing books for this child I loved long before his arrival in the material world, even when he lived entirely in the realm of the abstract, as the subject of late-night conversation with his mother, Pam—who, ever-vigilant in her commitment to the physical sciences, ensured that a periodic table of elements would adorn the wall of his nursery.

Each week of Pam's pregnancy came with its own revelation. We would look up, and suddenly he had a new weight (catalogued by a BabyCenter app on our phones which compared every new stage to a fruit or vegetable), and ears, and eyes, and a heartbeat that our midwife helped me to hear as I watched the FaceTime screen from a distance, in accordance with the hospital's pandemic protocol, nodding to the rhythm. We were taken aback by the data he provided each day. We learned early on, for example, that our son detested all manner of cold beverages and frozen confectionary delights. His consistency astonished us. Any strawberry Popsicles or bowls of chocolate ice cream were followed by a series of swift kicks in protest. The more we learned about him, the more we expanded the reading list. During the second ultrasound, he stuck his tongue out, which, as we are children of the early nineties, brought us to vintage images of Michael Jordan. Add a pop-up book about the NBA's golden age to the pile.

Almost all the books my parents gave me as a child were historical in nature and centered on folk heroes of some kind. My childhood shelves were packed with book-length profiles of Benjamin Banneker, George Washington Carver, Harriet Tubman, and Ida B. Wells, stories of all that African American people had collectively accomplished, conveyed symbolically through the triumphs of our champions. I needed to know them in order to know myself. This was part of my parents' comprehensive educational strategy for their children: the Modern School, my Sunday-school classroom, my entire South Yonkers neighborhood composed of families from across the African diaspora—poor and working people acting out, in word and practice, a vision of blackness that extended across a full spectrum of color, nationality, and language. These environments, not unlike the books in my room, instilled a sense that I had my own glorious place in the grand narrative of history. (Whatever lessons around the pervasiveness of American racism the books didn't accomplish, my father made up for with stories of integrating his high school in Jim Crow Alabama.) My skin, my hair, my eyes, my hands, my mind were lovely, loved, and I knew it. All were divinely crafted and were detested only by those who hated most else of what was wonderful in and about the world.

One of the more difficult parts of preparing to raise a black child in the United States of America—and it bears mentioning from the beginning that the joys are innumerable—is the question of where they will go to school. Most of us know, through both memory and a wealth of empirical data testifying to this difficult truth, that the classroom is a battleground. It is a site of struggle. It is a space in which, historically, our hair, our diction, our social practices have been denigrated as a matter of everyday protocol. The black aesthetic tradition, in one sense, is a single front in an ongoing war against this and other forms of asymmetrical violence against our children. In our poems and plays, stories and essays, we are mapping out a set of alternatives: another world, another way that things might eventually be if we are brave.

These days, when my mind turns toward these matters, I'm reminded of something Willie Perdomo said to me about legacy—about the importance of being a teacher and a beacon for his community. He told me, "The legacy for me would be . . . that somehow it is quite possible that a young boy who grew up in East Harlem in the late sixties through the seventies, through the eighties—that that young boy, because of his love of reading, because of the level of imagination that opened windows and rooftops and street corners and hallways and stoops, that that young poet could not only be a young poet from the block, could not only be the poet of the crew, but can go on to become the poet representing the whole state. And that there's someone out there looking at you and saying, 'Damn, Perdomo came from my block, and he's the state poet of New York along with Audre Lorde and Yusef Komunyakaa. In fact, he's the first Puerto Rican state poet of New York." Near the end of our conversation, Perdomo gestures toward inheritance, the immaterial gifts we pass along, the education that inheres in sharing our freedom dreams with the next generation. The cornerstone of his legacy, he says, "is the generations of poets that I have worked with over the last twenty-five years. Young poets who are now established poets. Urban Word kids who are now professors and teachers and instructors and published poets and analysts and scholars and so on. That's a legacy, because that's a whole 'nother block that you're hanging out on."

*

There is a playlist on my phone that's built entirely from the genius of John Coltrane, and I've been playing it for my son since the day he was born. It begins with Trane's cover of "My Favorite Things." In truth, I have no idea how the playlist ends, because we never get there. By the time we arrive at "Lush Life" or "Equinox" during the azure hours of the early morning, he's usually asleep again, or else we have decided that we're done dancing across the kitchen and are on to another activity. We have a few hours before Mom wakes up. The options unfold like a field before us. Most days, we move right from the dances to time with poems, as that feels like the most logical sequence. Early mornings, after all, are made for music.

Some recent favorites—and you should know that my sense of the work's reception is based on feedback in the form of ear-to-ear smiles, and yelling in the midst of one or more stanzas in direct succession—include Joy Priest's "Little Lamp," Al Young's "The Mountains of California: Part I," and "Something New Under the Sun" by Steve Scafidi. The Scafidi poem opens with the sentence "It would have to shine," and every one of the days that begins this way seems to. Even deep gray weather takes on new resonance: hours to spend watching sheets of rain re-arrange the backyard, making it much too muddy for Apollo 5 to play in. He doesn't always take this sort of shift in his routine well, Apollo, as he has recently had to adjust to having a new family member, and is still getting used to the feeling that not all of our attention is focused on him. This conundrum is mostly my fault. And in more ways than one, perhaps, naming him as I did for a god of poetry and light, a space shuttle, the theater where my mother first saw Smokey Robinson sing, and a cinematic revision of the greatest boxer of all time, his modern legacy renewed in the body of Michael B. Jordan. I'm named after a book in the Bible and an older brother who died before I was born. My mother takes her first name from her grandmother, and her second from the tall Puerto Rican nurse in the delivery room where my grandmother first guided her into the world.

My son, August Galileo, has a name that emerges from both African diaspora literature and a family commitment to studying the heavens. He is named for the legendary poet and playwright August Wilson as well as for Black August: the yearly commemorative event in which people all across the world celebrate not only the revolutionary legacy of George Jackson, who was slain on August 21, 1971, but also the practice of freedom across a much larger stretch of human history: the founding of the Underground Railroad, the Nat Turner rebellion, and the Haitian Revolution. *Galileo* is meant to gesture toward both the father of modern astronomy and the 1908 Fisk University speech delivered by W. E. B. Du Bois that bears his name: "Galileo Galilei." It is one of the most powerful pieces of oratory I have ever encountered. In it, Du Bois writes: "And you, graduates of Fisk University, are the watchmen on the outer wall. And you, Fisk University,

Intangible but real Personality, builded of Song and Sorrow, and the Spirits of Just Men made perfect, are as one standing Galileo—wise before the Vision of Death and the Bribe of the Lie."

Names are an incantation of a certain kind. *August Galileo* reminds us, and will hopefully remind our son, to have courage in the face of unthinkable odds. Persistence in the midst of the seemingly impossible. An unflinching dedication to wonder, respect for the essential drama of human life, and the ceremonies that make it worthwhile. The other big difference since August's arrival—aside from the new routine at sunrise—is that there are toys everywhere. Many of which have names that are not to be found on the boxes we purchased them in: the Wolf Throne (his swing), the Device (a gray baby sling), and the Rattle Snail (a rattle shaped just like a snail). This ever-expanding collective of objects makes it hard to walk through the living room, but a joy to be there. Once Mom comes downstairs, it's party time once again. We throw on a KAYTRANADA DJ set and dance until we are tired, falling to the couch in unison, where we rest for a while.

One of the great gifts of the black expressive tradition is that it refuses the notion of human immortality—especially as it is often imagined in our secular modernity, through private property or conquest—and yet gives you moments where you feel invincible, endless. We do not live forever. But we do live on. We live for the children. We engage in protracted struggle so that they might inherit a planet worthy of their loveliness.

While I once understood this largely in the abstract, this sense of things now animates my days. I can't hear Coltrane without thinking of my boy arriving here on a Sunday night, hours before dawn. Recently, while looking through old records, I found a copy of Trane's debut album with Atlantic, *Giant Steps*. It felt like a sign.

Around the same time, I discovered Michael S. Harper's 1970 collection of poems, *Dear John, Dear Coltrane*. There's a poem there, "Alone," that has been stuck in my head ever since I found it:

> A friend told me
> He'd risen above jazz
> I leave him there.[2]

Reading Harper, I am reminded that there's an unimpeachable beauty here, in the spaces where many say there is nothing to be studied, nothing to be learned or celebrated. In those interstices—the cafe, the community center, the poetry circus in the desert, the bar, the construction site, the open mic—line by line, brick by brick, we are inaugurating new worlds. Every time we touch the stage, we are reaching out to one another. We are stepping out, on trust, into the darkness, that our dreaming might be the bridge between us.

Acknowledgments

As it pertains to my life as a writer, the composition of this book has been an adventure without precedent or comparison. It has required—though I did not think of it this way at the outset—that I craft a kind of origin story. In order to do so, I had to reflect on the many disparate moments that helped to make some of the best parts of my present life possible. Thankfully, at every step, I had excellent company.

Thank you to my wife, Pam. This project has been in the works for a few years now, and I know I could not have seen it through without your patience and care. As I write this, having just put the final touches on the final draft of this book, you are in the living room with our son, August, watching *Blue's Clues*. I know all the songs by heart, because they have been a part of the soundtrack to our lives for the past two years, which have been filled with no shortage of joys. Whatever is good and true in this book, I know is the product of the support you have shown me, as I tried, and failed, and tried again to pull music from memory, and fuse many stories into one. Thanks for making the journey worthwhile.

Thank you to Henry Louis Gates Jr., for introducing me

to my incomparable agents, David Kuhn and Nate Muscato. And thank you, David and Nate, for taking a chance on an email introduction and introductory conversation in your office. Your confidence in me, and in this project, has meant a great deal.

To Toya: The first great writer and rhetorician I ever knew. I'm excited to see the new house, and look forward to celebrating with you soon (I'm writing this part in the month of August, so we're still a few weeks out). Thank you for pointing me, always, toward the good and the beautiful. And for never caging my voice. I wouldn't have made it here, to this moment, without you. Your quiet strength helped me survive.

To Mom and Dad: I hope the pages in this book reflect some measure of the depth of my respect and appreciation for you both. I am still only beginning to understand what you sacrificed in order to raise your children with dignity, and a real, unimpeachable sense that they could become whatever they wanted.

Thank you to my editor, Deb Garrison, for working tirelessly to help me bring this story to life. The work of an editor is truly singular, and I'm glad to have one with such an expansive vision, and discerning ear for language, on my side.

Sincerest thanks to my friends and colleagues for their continued support, especially in these turbulent times: Thomas Alston, Charlotte Bacon, Jamil Baldwin, Cory Benjamin, Everett Aaron Benjamin, Kyle Brooks, Jamall Calloway, Devin Chamberlain, Alex Chee, Daniel Claro, Ben Crossan, Tongo Eisen-Martin, Mary C. Fuller, Aracelis Girmay, Jarvis Givens, Bill Gleason, Carlos Andrés Gómez, Terrance Hayes,

R.A. Judy, Susan Lambe-Sariñana, Carvens Lissaint, Jesse McCarthy, Roshad Meeks, Isaac Miller, Ernie Mitchell, Wesley Morris, Timothy Pantoja, Gregory Pardlo, Imani Perry, Theri Pickens, Samora Pinderhughes, Elaine Scarry, Christina Sharpe, Tracy K. Smith, Law Smithson, Josef Sorett, Matthew Spellberg, Brandon Terry, Daniella Toosie-Watson, and Simone White.

Thank you to the Whiting Foundation, the John Simon Guggenheim Memorial Foundation, the Society of Fellows at Harvard University, and the Department of English and Creative Writing at Dartmouth College for the various forms of institutional support that helped make this manuscript possible.

Thank you to the archivists at the Center for Puerto Rican Studies at Hunter College for welcoming me, and for making room. I can't imagine this book without you all.

Thank you to my slam teammates and coaches from 2006 to 2009: Ben Alisuag, Hasan Malik Babb, Michael Cirelli, Gregory Corbin (for both BNV *and* IWPS, I didn't forget!), Aysha el-Shamayleh, Alysia Harris, Jamila Lyiscott, Caroline Rothstein, Sruthi Sadhujan, Tahani Salah, Noel Scales, Jason Henry Simon-Bierenbaum, and Chloe Wayne.

Thank you to my Strivers Row family, and all our supporters, for helping me build a life with poems.

Thank you to Stan Lathan, for believing.

Thank you to Sam Cook, Mark Eleveld, Sandra María Esteves, Dylan Garity, Carlos Andrés Gomez, Bob Holman, Tyehimba Jess, Michael Mlekoday, Willie Perdomo, Jive Poetic, Caroline Rothstein, Patricia Smith, Lauren Whitehead, Saul Williams, and all of the other poets I interviewed for this book. Your openness was an education.

And a special shout-out to everyone out there still brave enough to sign up for an open mic or poetry slam at your local venue. You give purpose and breath to this art form.

Notes

Book 1: The Nuyoricans

1. Miguel Algarín, "His Cafe Is Alive with the Spoken Word," interview between Algarín and David Berreby, *Newsday*, December 5, 1990.

2. Pedro Pietri, "Puerto Rican Obituary," *Monthly Review* 56, no. 2 (204): 48.

3. *Nuyorican Poetry: An Anthology of Puerto Rican Words and Feelings* (New York: Morrow, 1975), 15.

4. Carmen Dolores Hernández, *Puerto Rican Voices in English: Interviews with Writers* (Westport: Praeger, 1997).

5. Ibid.

6. William Shakespeare *The Oxford Shakespeare: Richard II.* (New York: Oxford University Press, 2011).

7. Miguel Algarín, *Love Is Hard Work: Memorias de Loisaida/Poems* (New York: Simon and Schuster, 1997).

8. *Nuyorican Poetry*, 15.

9. Ibid, 10.

10. Hernández, Carmen Dolores Hernández, *Puerto Rican Voices in English: Interviews with Writers* (London: Praeger, 1997), 41.

11. Nina Siegal, "Neighborhood Report: Harlem; After a Sale, School's Future Is Uncertain," *The New York Times*, August 8, 1999, 6.

12. Ibid.

13. Imani Perry, *May We Forever Stand: A History of the Black National Anthem* (Chapel Hill: University of North Carolina Press, 2018).

14. Ibid.

15. Paul Laurence Dunbar, "We wear the mask," *Lyrics of Lowly Life* (1896).

16. James Baldwin, "How to Cool It," *Esquire*, August 2, 2017.

17. Gwendolyn Brooks, "The Blackstone Rangers," *In the Mecca: Poems* (New York: Harper & Row, 1968).

18. Langston Hughes, "Let America Be America Again," *Présence Africaine* 59 (1966): 3–5.

19. Amiri Baraka, "The Black Arts Movement: Its Meaning and Potential," *Journal of Contemporary African Art*, no. 29 (2011): 26.

20. Derek Walcott, *The Poetry of Derek Walcott 1948–2013* (New York: Farrar, Straus and Giroux, 2014), 260.

21. Carter G. Woodson, *The Mis-Education of the Negro* (San Diego: Book Tree, 2006).

22. Amiri Baraka and William J. Harris, "An Interview with Amiri Baraka," *The Greenfield Review*, 1980.

23. Nikki Giovanni, *Conversations with Nikki Giovanni* (University Press of Mississippi, 1992), 119.

24. Zora Neale Hurston, "Characteristics of Negro Expression," in *African American Literary Theory: A Reader*, ed. Winston Napier (New York: New York University Press, 2000).

25. Leon Ichaso, "Leon Ichaso," interview by Lynn Geller, *BOMB Magazine*, January 1, 2002.

26. Ibid.

27. Miguel Piñero, Miguel, *La Bodega Sold* [????] (Arte Público Press, 1980).

28. Lauren Berlant, *Cruel Optimism*, (Durham, NC: Duke University Press, 2011).

29. Algarín, *Love Is Hard Work*.

30. Ed Morales, *Living in Spanglish: The Search for Latino Identity in America* (New York: St. Martin's Griffin, 2002).

31. Thomas Swiss, "Sweet Nothings: An Anthology of Rock and Roll in American Poetry." *Popular Music* 15, no. 2 (1996): 233–240.

32. Ibid.

33. "Miguel Piñero and Miguel Algarín Harmonizing," *Fried Shoes Cooked Diamonds*, directed by Costanzo Allione (1979: Mystic Fire Video, 1998).

Book 2: The Birth of Slam Poetry

1. Saul Williams, Saul, "Amethyst Rocks," *The Spoken Word Revolution: Slam, Hip Hop, and The Poetry of a New Generation* (2003): 55–57.

2. Ludwig Wittgenstein, *Philosophical Investigations* (Wiley, 2010), 5.

3. Susan Stewart, *Cinder: New and Selected Poems.* (Graywolf Press, 2017), 91.

4. Amalio Madueno, Peter Rabbit, and Terry Jacobus, *Taos Poetry Circus: The Nineties.* (Pennywhistle Press, 2002).

5. Marc Smith, *Take the Mic: The Art of Performance Poetry, Slam, and the Spoken Word* (Naperville: Sourcebooks MediaFusion, 2009), 22.

6. Evelyn McDonnell, "Blood of a Poet: Paul Beatty Puts the New Poetry in Your Face," *The Village Voice* (May 1, 1990).

7. Marc Kelly Smith and Joe Kraynak, *The Complete Idiot's Guide to Slam Poetry* (Indianapolis: Alpha Books, 2004), 14–15.

8. Ibid.

9. Ibid.

10. Ibid.

11. Patricia Smith, *Teahouse of the Almighty* (Coffee House Press, 2013).

12. Marc Kelly Smith, *Ground Zero: A Collection of Chicago Poems,* (Northwestern University Press, 2020).

13. Mara Veitch, "Earl Sweatshirt Tells Ta-Nehisi Coates About His Cultural Trust Fund," *Interview* (April 27, 2022).

14. Rick Kogan, "Marc Smith Celebrates 25 Years of Poetry Slams," *Chicago Tribune,* July 17, 2011.

15. Pedro Pietri, *Traffic Violations* (Maplewood, NJ: Waterfront Press, 1983), 103.

16. Bob Kaufman, *The Ancient Rain* (New York: New Directions, 1981), ix.

17. Adam Sandler, "MTV Sponsors Tour of Poets," *Variety* (February 1, 1994).

18. Audre Lorde, "The Transformation of Silence into Language and Action." *Identity Politics in the Women's Movement* (1977): 82.

19. Susan Weinstein, *The Room Is on Fire: The History, Pedagogy, and Practice of Youth Spoken Word Poetry* (State University of New York Press, 2018), 85.

20. Toni Morrison, *The Source of Self-regard: Selected Essays, Speeches, and Meditations* (New York: Alfred A. Knopf, 2019), 57.

Epilogue in Three Parts: The Hill We Climb,
Summertime, A Few of My Favorite Things

1. Michael S. Harper, *Dear John, Dear Coltrane,* (University of Pittsburgh Press, 1970).

2. Shayla Love, "*Hamilton* Star Daveed Diggs: 'Slam Poetry Saved My Life,'" *The Washington Post*, July 18, 2016.

Index

ILLUSTRATION CREDITS

TEXT PERMISSIONS